Poems Seven

POEMS SEVEN

New and Complete Poetry

Alan Dugan

● ● ● ● ● ● ●

SEVEN STORIES PRESS

New York : London : Toronto : Sydney

First trade paperback edition: September 2002

Carl Phillips's foreword was adapted from his introduction of Alan Dugan at the Fine Arts Work Center in Provincetown, Mass., on the evening of July 20, 2001.

Seven Stories Press
140 Watts Street
New York NY 10013
http://www.sevenstories.com

In Canada:
Hushion House, 36 Northline Road, Toronto, Ontario M4B 3E2

In the U.K.:
Turnaround Publisher Services Ltd., Unit 3, Olympia Trading Estate, Coburg Road, Wood Green, London N22 6TZ

In Australia:
Tower Books, 9/19 Rodborough Road, Frenchs Forest NSW 2086

Library of Congress Cataloging-in-Publication Data

Dugan, Alan
    Poems seven: new and complete poetry / Alan Dugan.—A Seven Stories Press 1st ed.
        p. cm.
    ISBN 1-58322-265-0
    ISBN 1-58322-512-9 pbk.
      I. Title.
    PS3554.U33 P65 2001
    811'.54—dc21

                                                        2001041089

9 8 7 6 5 4

College professors may order examination copies of Seven Stories Press titles for a free six-month trial period. To order, visit www.sevenstories.com/textbook, or fax on school letterhead to (212) 226-1411.

Book design by M. Astella Saw
Printed in the U.S.A.

CONTENTS

Poems Two (1963)

Poems Three (1967)

Poems Four (1974)

Poems Five (1983)

Poems Six (1989)

Poems Seven (New poems)

The first time I ever heard Dugan read was in 1989, and it was also the first time I'd ever read *my* poetry in public—at the old Fire House in Wellfleet, where Dugan and all of us in his Castle Hill poetry workshop read together at the end of summer. Dugan read a poem whose first lines are these: "After your first poetry reading/I shook hands with you/and got a hard-on. Thank you." Six weeks earlier, I'd have been shocked. But by then, I'd learned already that—as a poet and as a teacher—Dugan was nothing if not direct: exactingly, and often disarmingly so. It helps to remember that this is a poet whose every book has had essentially the same title—*Poems*—from the first volume, *Poems*, to this *Poems Seven: New and Complete Poetry*. Dugan's commitment to truth and his refusal to adorn or shroud that truth in distracting ornament have been his most important lessons for me, even as they continue to be a necessary presence in contemporary American poetry. So much of poetry handles the world in one of two ways: there's the flee-in-the-face-of-conundrum approach, known as "transcendent;" and there's the construct-your-own-alternative-world approach—I believe it too calls itself transcendent. Dugan works differently. As he says in "Against a Sickness: To the Female Double Principle God," "My visions/are not causal but final:/there's no place to go to/but on." For Dugan, existential angst is irrelevant—it's all existence, nothing to hope for beyond, so no reason to rush *toward* that beyond, and no reason to despair as to what will happen later, because nothing *will*. His is a queerly, bracingly sobering sense of reality—in the spirit of Lucretius, instructive and, in a weird way, comforting, if we know enough to laugh at the absurdity that, for Dugan, is less the human predicament than simply what it is to be human. And what the poems do is help us not toward a solution for our wrestling with a life but toward a realistic vision of the wrestling itself.

But if Lucretian, then also Whitmanian, a sheer revelery in the high and low, squalor and joy: sure, Dugan frequently starts at and responds to such Classical forebears as Virgil, Heraclitus, Tyrtaeus, and Plutarch—but we also come up against Dynaflo, the reduction of Orpheus and Rilke to mere prigs, and the chance to understand the idea of God by becoming God, essentially, via masturbation, about which Dugan says (in "For Masturbation"): "THIS IS THE WAY IT IS, and if/it is a "terrible disgrace"/it is as I must will." In the world we've come to know as Dugan's Edge, all is flux, everything comes with its disorienting but finally illuminating flipside; the very wind that sweeps a lover's hair has known the foul smell of the dead on a distant battle-field; a little girl's response to being stripped for rape is a simple, comic exclamation of "Wow."

In "American Against Solitude," Dugan tells us "it's in the Close of life/that towering Virtù happens. Why/be absent from the wheeling world?/It is an education." The gift of Dugan's poems is their clarity of vision, yes, but also their encouragement to us to walk straight into the thick of the truth–to "walk out bravely into the daily accident," as Dugan has put it. If life is all an act of falling, Dugan suggests a foun-tain as a possible model from which to learn to fall with grace—which means not resisting but embracing the here-and-now, risking the unknown, because (as Dugan says) it "might be serious, dangerous, and worth it." Even as his poems are, for what they show us of ourselves.

Dugan's many honors include the Pulitzer Prize, the National Book Award, the Prix de Rome, the Shelley Memorial Award, and an Award in Literature from the American Academy and Institute of Arts and Letters. But all of that seems somehow incidental. It's my sense that Dugan would have written anyway, always has, and still does for the simple reason that he must: a kind of instinct—as has always been, also, his generosity to his students, his belief in particular in new voices, and his ability to help a new voice first to know and then to trust itself. I'm but one such beneficiary, but so are all of Dugan's students and all who have had the good fortune to work and grow at the Fine Arts Work Center and the Castle Hill Center for the Arts, of both of which Dugan

POEMS
(1961)

THIS MORNING HERE

This is this morning: all
the evils and glories of last night
are gone except for their
effects: the great world wars
I and II, the great marriage
of Edward the VII or VIII
to Wallis Warfield Simpson and
the rockets numbered like the Popes
have incandesced in flight
or broken on the moon: now
the new day with its famous
beauties to be seized at once
has started and the clerks
have swept the sidewalks
to the curb, the glass doors
are open, and the first
customers walk up and down
the supermarket alleys of their eyes
to Muzak. Every item has
been cut out of its nature,
wrapped disguised as something
else, and sold clean by fractions.
Who can multiply and conquer
by the Roman numbers? Lacking
the Arab frenzy of the zero, they
have obsolesced: the butchers
have washed up and left
after having killed and dressed
the bodies of the lambs all night,
and those who never have seen blood awake

ON AN EAST WIND FROM THE WARS

The wind came in for several thousand miles all night
and changed the close lie of your hair this morning. It
has brought well-travelled sea-birds who forget
their passage, singing. Old songs from the old
battle- and burial-grounds seem new in new lands.
They have to do with spring as new in seeming as
the old air idling in your hair in fact. So new,
so ignorant of any weather not your own,
you like it, breathing in a wind that swept
the battlefields of their worst smells, and took the dead
unburied to the potter's field of air. For miles
they sweetened on the sea-spray, the foul washed off,
and what is left is spring to you, love, sweet,
the salt blown past your shoulder luckily. No
wonder your laugh rings like a chisel as it cuts
your children's new names in the tombstone of thin air.

ON AN OLD ADVERTISEMENT AND AFTER A
PHOTOGRAPH BY ALFRED STIEGLITZ

The formal, blooded stallion, the Arabian,
will stand for stud at fifty bucks a throw,
but there is naturally a richer commerce in his act,
eased in this instance by a human palm
and greased with money: the quiver in his haunch
is not from flies, no; the hollow-sounding,
kitten-crushing hooves are sharp and blind,
the hind ones hunting purchase while the fore
rake at the mare's flank of the sky.
Also, the two- or three-foot prick that curls
the mare's lip back in solar ectasy
is greater than the sum of its desiring:
the great helm of the glans, the head
of feeling in the dark, is what spits out,
beyond itself, its rankly generative cream.
After that heat, the scraggled, stallion-legged foal
is not as foolish as his acts: the bucking and
the splayed-out forelegs while at grass
are practices: he runs along her flank
in felt emergencies, inspired by love to be
his own sweet profit of the fee and the desire,
compounded at more interest than the fifty in the bank.

PHILODENDRON

Drinking Song: An Indoor Plant: A Dull Life   *GLOSS*

The person of this plant with heart-shaped leaves
and off-shot stalks, bending at each knee,
is built of dishwater, cigarette smoke, no
sunlight, and humus mixed with peat-moss. Like
genius, it survives our inattention and the dark,
potted like myself indoors, and goes on growing.
It grows for no known cause that I can find
outside itself, by means of mumbling, flowering
no flowers, no flowers, none for all these years.

Balance and survival: it has
a strategy of elbows as
it breaks its hairy knees
while climbing up the wall
and then juts off again,
shaped like a claw.

Since imagination has the answer to these noes,
imagine it as one of those survivors in the old
swamps, shadowed by the grown, light-headed conifers:
fit for the damps, whose gentlest odor seems
corrosive, mightily akin to older, shadowed ferns,
it might have dropped its pollen in the black
water where the pollen swam, and thus become
perseverant in going on in lust, like us,
and mobile through its young. Even now

Even at its top most
broken elbow, it
must turn uprooted from
its heaven in the air,
and, in going down,
not find it on the floor,

it does move on in time, too, each elbow putting out
a stalk and leaf in faith and doubt, but no
flowers. Who knows what in hell it loves or lacks
as crawler in arrest. Sometimes to water it,
to notice it, to keep it out of the bureau drawer
and trained to climb perennially around itself,
is piety enough toward indoor plants right now
when one is thirsty, too, for rich lost tastes
and light streaming down through amniotic air.

either. Compelled to move
anyhow, it always has
an angle and an out
in going nowhere, all
around itself
in faith and doubt.

6

PRISON SONG

The skin ripples over my body like moon-wooed water,
rearing to escape me. Where would it find another
animal as naked as this one it hates to cover?
Once it told me what was happening outside,
who was attacking, who caressing, and what the air
was doing to feed or freeze me. Now I wake up
dark at night, in a textureless ocean of ignorance,
or fruit bites back and water bruises like a stone:
a jealousy, because I look for other tools to know
with, and another armor, better fitted to my flesh.
So, let it lie, turn off its clues, or try to leave:
sewn on me seamless like those painful shirts
the body-hating saints wore, this sheath of hell
is pierced to my darkness nonetheless: what traitors
labor in my face, what hints they smuggle through
its itching guard! But even in the night it jails,
with nothing but its lies and silences to feed upon,
the jail itself can make a scenery, sing prison songs
and set off fireworks to praise a homemade day.

IMPERIAL SONG FOR WARMTH

Snow that makes graces on a soldier's sleeve
is ordered rain, the crystal wheels
each agony is strapped to in his business:
waiting in the lee of enemies.
The rain that duplicates forever
can make news again,
distinction in each flake,
but snow is not his order, ordering.

The lesser orders, like the ants,
the spiders, and platoons of snow,
make wholes by ruined parts:
frozen in wait, or jungled monkey-wise,
they organize by jeopardies,
atrocious in design.
Oh web, geometry of appetite,
oh darkly ordered, muted ants,
the snow is not in order, ordering.

Fire and ice burn unalike:
the flakes have touches for his skin,
his eyebrows, and the hair
his hand is aped with; what
exasperation of survival that the snow,
with careful walking,
cracks like the salt in the boot
or infiltrates more loving warmth.
Baled in rags
and like a haystack, warm at heart,
unhurt he is a center of decay,

but once the heat is hurt,
the snow for lashes, dusted on his eyes,
will fill his wrinkles of fatigue
with tracery, will cover him to death
with tracery, a thread of shuttles
webbed to net a death. Oh air,
diamond of ice,
the wound is mammoth, fixed in glacial ice:
its trivial grimace will bloom
as rotten ice at thaw.

So which is better, to campaign
between the Tropics where
immediate bulbs of sweat
flower in stains on his fatigues
and rot the living, or among
geodesic spiders of ice?
The latter children nest in a grotesque,
but southward, with the butcher ants,
the death does not
go uniformed in flesh all winter long,
far from the monkey's eulogy,
nor do the wheels of snow
bunch in the lee of his crystal ear
and hum the umbra's note:
Earth makes night, snow is black
in ordering his brain to stop.

THE SO-CALLED WILD HORSES OF THE WATER

The so-called wild horses of the water
stumbled all over the boulders
and fell steaming and foaming over
the world's edge down the roaring
white way of the waterfall
into the black pool of the death
of motion at the bottom where
the cold stoned water lay
dense as a diamond of pressure and
the eye of silence stared unmoved
at the world's cavalry falling in
to be the seer not the heard again.

SIXTEEN LINES ON MARCHING

In spring when the ego arose from the genitals
after a winter's refrigeration, the sergeants
were angry: it was a time of looking
to the right and left instead of straight ahead.

Now the rich lost tastes have been lost again,
the green girls grown brown for another year:
intelligent bodies make ready for the entropy begun
by north winds and the declination of the sun.

Say death, soldiering, or fear: these words
are luxuries no more but the true words of winter
when the flesh hardens and collects itself around
the skeleton to protect what little it contains.

If anything is to happen let it happen now.
If anything is expected of us let the orders be cut
immediately and read Winter; the proper season
for caution. Match, if you can, its coldness: spring.

LANDFALL

The curtains belly in the waking room.
Sails are round with holding, horned at top,
and net a blue bull in the wind: the day.
They drag the blunt hulls of my heels awake
and outrigged by myself through morning seas.
If I do land, let breakfast harbor me.

Waking in June, I found a first fruit
riding out the water on a broken branch.
Sleep was a windfall, and its floating seeds
steered me among the Cyclades of noise.
A coastal woman with a cricket in her hair
took soundings as the time chirped in her head:
I knew that night-time is an Island District;
curtains are my sails to shore.
Block and tackle string a butcher's dance
to hoist the sun on home: the bull
is beached and hung to dry, and through
his bloody noon, the island of his flank
quakes in the silence and disturbs the flies.

Flesh has crawled out on the beach of morning,
salt-eyed, with the ocean wild in hair,
and landed, land-locked, beached on day,
must hitch its hand to traces and resist
the fierce domestic horses teamed to it.

Drivers and driven both, the plowing heels
bloody the furrows after plunging beasts:
the spring of day is fleshed for winter fruit.

Fallen in salt-sweat, piercing skin, the bones
essay plantation in their dirt of home

and rest their aching portion in the heat's
blood afternoon. O if the sun's day-laborer
records inheritable yield, the script
is morning's alpha to omega after dark:
the figured head to scrotum of the bull.

Accountancy at sundown is the wine of night:
walking the shore, I am refreshed by it
and price the windrise and the bellowing surf
while, waiting for its freight of oil and hides,
a first sail starts the wind by snapping whips.

LOVE SONG: I AND THOU

Nothing is plumb, level, or square:
    the studs are bowed, the joists
are shaky by nature, no piece fits
    any other piece without a gap
or pinch, and bent nails
    dance all over the surfacing
like maggots. By Christ
    I am no carpenter. I built
the roof for myself, the walls
    for myself, the floors
for myself, and got
    hung up in it myself. I
danced with a purple thumb
    at this house-warming, drunk
with my prime whiskey: rage.
    Oh I spat rage's nails
into the frame-up of my work:
    it held. It settled plumb,
level, solid, square and true
    for that great moment. Then
it screamed and went on through,
    skewing as wrong the other way.
God damned it. This is hell,
    but I planned it, I sawed it,
I nailed it, and I
    will live in it until it kills me.
I can nail my left palm
    to the left-hand crosspiece but
I can't do everything myself.
    I need a hand to nail the right,
a help, a love, a you, a wife.

IMPORTATION OF LANDSCAPES

The seed of an iron flower
must grow in gravel
or else make its own
if it is taken from the desert
and sunk in loam.
What a hard garden,
lovers: iron is used
to the routine of oil
but gets the bloody rust
in damp: there, the oasis,
a devotion in the sand,
prays flesh, virus to mammoth,
and supports them all,
but when the regular iron
flowers in sensuous ease
it languishes; the bloom
weeps dust. Spear-shaped,
venomous as plows were thought to be,
the leaves fall sick
and make a desert: iron's
oasis in delight
and field of strength.

THE NATURAL ENEMIES OF THE CONCH

1

The first point of the shell
was moored to zero but
its mouth kissed one
and paid in torque.
A turbine in the conch
is whirled so fast
that it stands still,
humming with cold light.

2

The animal inside
is out of luck in art.
Tourists gouge him out
of water's Gabriel
and gild the whirling horn
to make a lamp of home.
The death, a minor surf,
sounds in the living room.

3

(That's the way it is
with the ugly: ugliness
should arm their flesh
against the greedy but
they grow such wiles
around the hurt

that estheticians come
with love, apology,
and knives and cut
the beauty from the quick.)

4

The Maya crack the gem
where muscles glue
the palace to the slug
and eat him out. Again
the curio is fleshed
but wrecked like Knossos
with a window down the maze
toward nothing
where a bull at heart
roars in the start of surf.

5

(To know why slime
should build such forts,
challenge the tooth
one pod is spurred with.
He has a tongue on guard,
like authors, out around
the works, and can retreat
in what reveals him,
claw last, at a touch.)

6

Turned in his likeness
like a foraging son,
there is a Natural Drill
that bores a vent in him
and taps his life.
Like Prince Hippolytus,
when we behave too
simply toward some law
we have our image,
father, from the sea:
the sea-bull bellowing
to foul our traces,
dragging us to death
behind disturbed machines.

7

The snail retreats to nothing
where the shell is born,
pearl of its phlegm and rock,
small as water can whirl.
Whorling down the turns
from mouth to point,
it points in vanishing
to university,
where thickened water learned
one graph with nebulae
and turned the living horn
on zero's variable lathe.

8

It voids the plum, wrack
and accidents of space
and sounds a sea-bull
first ashore. Similar ears,
listening mouth to mouth,
hear it as ocean's time
and turn into the brain
as mirrors of the maze.

PORTRAIT

The captive flourished like
a mushroom in his oubliette.
He breathed his night's breath every day,
took food and water from the walls
and ruled his noisy rats and youth.
He made a calendar of darkness,
thought his boredom out, and carved
Heaven in his dungeon with a broken spoon.

At last he made his own
light like a deep sea fish, and when
his captors' children came for him
they found no madman in a filthy beard
or heap of rat-picked bones:
they found a spry, pale old gentleman
who had a light around his head.
Oh he could stare as well as ever,
argue in a passionate voice
and walk on to the next
detention in their stone dismay
unaided.

OASIS

Whelped from blackness by a pressure of rocks,
black water rose like breath from the lungs
and burst in speech. It poured its glitter,
trouble, on the sand, and babbled on about
its quick exploits in shape above the plain.
This speaking taught the desert thirst: once
sucked at by that thirster, sand, the water spread
its cool hair over fever: sand was changed:
what was almost sand in sand, the waiting sand,
a hidden seed, leaped up and burst in palms!
The water argued greenery to sand: now sand
is passionate with fruit! Ticking with bugs,
bustling with flowers and death, the garden is
a place and fireworks, a green wild on the calm.

Oh its mirages offer water, figs, and shade
to windrift birds for songs and wings of praise.
Clock-lost nomads, lost in the running sands,
will have to choose, when madness lights
advertisements of water to their soaking need,
if they will drop to the truth of desert, dry
to sand, or run to where the fanfare of quick
water winds their clocks, gives place to love,
and lets them drink their living from its deaths.

WHAT HAPPENED? WHAT DO YOU EXPECT?

The waiter waited, the cook ate,
the scales read zero, and the clock
began to agree. It agreed
and disagreed but rang no bells,
and in the quiet of the whole
peeled onion on the chopping block
the whole flayed lamb stamped
     QUALITY
hung by its heels and was
devoured by a fly. Outside,
a woman screamed and stopped.
Two cops came in for coffee-and,
laughing and filling the place
with night as black as the sweat
in the armpits of their shirts.
"Some guy hit his girl friend
and she didn't like it or us
either." Oh it had been
the countdown for a great
catastrophe that had not
happened, not as raw event,
but as time in the death of the lamb.

ON HURRICANE JACKSON

Now his nose's bridge is broken, one eye
will not focus and the other is a stray;
trainers whisper in his mouth while one ear
listens to itself, clenched like a fist;
generally shadowboxing in a smoky room,
his mind hides like the aching boys
who lost a contest in the Panhellenic games
and had to take the back roads home,
but someone else, his perfect youth,
laureled in newsprint and dollar bills,
triumphs forever on the great white way
to the statistical Sparta of the champs.

POEM

The person who can do
accounts receivable as fast
as steel machines and out-
talk telephones, has wiped
her business lipstick off,
undone her girdle and belts,
and stepped down sighing from
the black quoins of her heels
to be the quiet smiler with
changed eyes. After long-
haired women have unwired
their pencil-pierced buns, it's an
event with pennants when
the Great Falls of emotion say
that beauty is in residence,
grand in her hotel of flesh,
and Venus of the marriage manual,
haloed by a diaphragm,
steps from the shell *Mercenaria*
to her constitutional majesty
in the red world of love.

Imagine that the fast life of a bird
sang in the branches of the cold
cast-off antlers of a stag
and lit the points of bone
with noises like St. Elmo's fire.
Worn, those antlers were
an outer counterweight,
extravagant in air and poised
against a branching need
drumming in the red inside
the arteries or antlers of the heart.
That was the balance that allowed
the stag's head's limber rise,
and might have been the gift
the temporary, reed-boned bird
sang air about: abundance,
rank beyond the need. The horns
appear before the eye to be
more permanent than songs
that branch out lightly on the air
or root into the chest
as singing's negative, the breath,
that touches at the branching veins
at depth:
but when the leaping rut
slept growing in the hollow of the hind,
the candelabra that the head
dazzled the wedding with
guttered to rubbish and were cast.
That perch for calls and bird-

song was a call itself,
and fell to grace the wilds
correctly, since an itch,
under the rootholds of the horns,
whitens with mushroom wants
in cellars of the antlers' nerves
just off the brain,
and wants to make its many points again.

Once cast, they are the dead and fall
duly as a sound falls in the cool
of smoking days, when air
sags with the damp and song
swirls in the hollows: this
is so the works can start again,
untrammeled by the done, downed
wonders, and be upstart news
to publicize the crocus of next spring.
The stag had something on his mind
beside his wants, and it
is more than curious, the way
the horns are worn at ease
by cranial fulcrums, since the like of them,
the lighter songs or battle-cries of birds,
hum in the chambers of the nose
just off the brain,
so that the chambered mute, the brain,
silent in wants and plans,
vibrates in closest sympathy
with what is not its own

and plays as best it can.
Those were the works,
the prides and hat-trees of the head
that climbed out of the brain
to show its matter: earth, and how a beast
who wears a potted plant, all thorns,
is mostly desert, plus a glory
unsustained. Oh it
is useless in a fight
won by the head and heels,
not nicety, not war-cries worn
in silence to be seen. The hinds,
cropping the perimeter of war,
sooner accept the runnel one
who has not fronded his desire
with public works. Call and be gone,
bird: the one who wears the horns
can bear the singer too, mindlessly singing all
the bird-brained airs of spring,
but has to cast the tuning forks
that let the eye see song,
and winter with this loss.

The bone as singing-post
is capital enough in arms
to hold the nation of your sound
in singing's fief: the brain's
savage receptionist, the ear,
beating a drum outside its closest door,
joins with the civil eye's

electrical distance from the brain
in witnessing the poles of prongs and sounds
arcing across their earthworks of desire:
the sounds and tines
must be some excess of the flesh
that wants beyond efficiency
in time, but cannot find
much permanence outside it: getting or not aside,
it must branch out in works
that cap itself, for some
imaginary reason out of mind.

PORTRAIT

He wore the burnt-cork moustache and coonskin cap
that all the other boy pirate captains wore
in the comic strips, and when he smiled, real
Douglas Fairbanks diamonds glittered in his eyes
and teeth, but the first mate knew that he
was worried about his father: the fine old
gentleman, chuckling, firm, but kind,
had not been seen for several episodes.
Then it became clear: behind his smiles
and flashing gallantry there were two
serious drives: 1. Concern for the lost father,
and: 2. Worship of fuel as a god,
whether of gas or air, to drive or sail
him forward, always forward in the search,
although the old man had been dropped astern.

MEMORIAL SERVICE FOR THE INVASION BEACH
WHERE THE VACATION IN THE FLESH IS OVER

I see that there it is on the beach. It is
ahead of me and I walk toward it: its
following vultures and contemptible dogs
are with it, and I walk toward it. If,
in the approach to it, I turn my back
to it, then I walk backwards: I
approach it as a limit. Even if I fall
to hands and knees, I crawl to it.
Backwards or forwards I approach it.

There is the land on one hand, rising, and
the ocean on the other, falling away;
what the sky does, I can not look to see,
but it's around, as ever, all around.
The courteous vultures move away in groups
like functionaries. The dogs circle and stare
like working police. One wants a heel
and gets it. I approach it, concentrating so
on not approaching it, going so far away
that when I get there I am sideways like
the crab, too limited by carapace to say:

"Oh here I am arrived, all; yours today."
No: kneeling and facing away, I will
fall over backwards in intensity of life
and lie convulsed, downed struggling,
sideways even, and should a vulture ask
an eye as its aperitif, I grant it,
glad for the moment wrestling by a horse
whose belly has been hollowed from the rear,

who's eyeless. The wild dog trapped in its ribs
grins as it eats its way to freedom. Not
conquered outwardly, and after rising once,
I fall away inside, and see the sky around
rush out away into the vulture's craw
and barely can not hear them calling, "Here's one."

Ireland was better in its dream,
with the oppressor foreign.
Now its art leaves home to keen
and its voice is orange.
It is a sad revolt, for loving's health,
that beats its enemy and then itself.

Now that Irishmen are free
to enslave themselves together
they say that it is better they
do worst to one another
then have the english do them good
in an exchange of joy for blood.

A just as alien pius blacks
their greens of lovers' commerce;
rehearsing victory, they lack
a government to fill its promise.
Worse, law has slacked the silly harp
that was their once and only Ark

out, and I am sorry to be flip
and narrowly disrespectful,
but since I wade at home in it
I stoop and take a mouthful
to splatter the thick walls of their heads
with American insult! Irish sense is dead.

WEEDS AS PARTIAL SURVIVORS

The chorus of the weeds, unnameably
profuse, sings Courage, Courage, like
an India of unemployables who have
no other word to say and say it.
Too bendable to break, bowing away
together from the wind although
the hail or hurricane can knock them flat,
they rise up wet by morning. This
morning erection of the weeds
is not so funny: It
is perseverance dancing: some of them,
the worst, are barely rooted and
a lady gardener can pull them out
ungloved. Nevertheless, they do do
what they do or die, surviving all
catastrophes except the human: they
extend their glosses, like the words I said,
on sun-cracked margins of the sown
lines of our harrowed grains.

THE MIRROR PERILOUS

I guess there is a garden named
"Garden of Love." If so, I'm in it:
I am the guesser in the garden.
There is a notice by the central pond
that reads: "Property of Narcissus.
Trespass at your own risk,"
so I went there. That is where,
having won but disdained a lady,
he fell for his own face and died,
rightly, "not having followed through,"
as the sentence read, read by the lady:
Oh you could hear her crying all about
the wilderness and wickedness of law.
I looked in that famous mirror perilous
and it wasn't much: my own face,
beautiful, and at the bottom,
bone, a rusty knife, two beads,
and something else I cannot name.
I drank my own lips on the dare
but could not drink the lips away.
The water was heavy, cool, and clear,
but did not quench. A lady laughed
behind my back; I learned the worst:
I could take it or leave it, go or stay,
and went back to the office drunk,
possessed of an echo but not a fate.

LETTER TO EVE

The lion and lioness are intractable,
the leaves are covered with dust,
and even the peacocks will not
preen. You should come back,
burnish us with your former look,
and let the search for truth
go. After a loud sleep last night
I got up late and saw a new
expression on the faces of the deer;
the shrews and wolves are gaunt
and out of sorts: they nosed
their usual fruits and do not know
what they intend to do. The dogs
got tangled up in an unusual way:
one put its urinary tube
into the other's urinary tract
and could not get it out.
Standing tail to tail for hours,
they looked at me with wise,
supplicatory eyes. I named
two new sounds: snarl and shriek,
and hitherto unnoticed bells,
which used to perform the air,
exploded!, making a difference.
Come back before the garden does
what I'll call "die," not that it
matters. Rib, Rib, I have a new
opinion of your Eve, called "lust"
or Love, I don't know which,
and want to know how I will choose.

AGAINST FRANCE: ON THE ALGERIAN
PLEASURES OF ENTITY

When I died the devils tortured me with icepicks and pliers
and all the other instruments they learned from men of faith;
they took off my genitals and nails, less troubles, chained me
to the wall, and came in shifts with forced foods and electrodes.

Later, after works, I tore the chains from the wall. What whips
chains are! I lashed my lashers and escaped their cell,
armed to my last two teeth in search of god. My arms, though,
were chains chained to my arms, so what I touched I struck.

I met all the animals with beaks and offered them myself
to rend, since, as a student of torture, I had found it fun,
and wrecked them as they bit. What would I have done
if I had met a smile? Well, I swam the river of spit,

crossed a plain of scorpions, and went into the lake
of fire. I emerged bone, dripping the last of my flesh,
a good riddance, and asked whoever came to chew the bones,
"Where is god?" Each answered: "Here I am, now. I am,

in a way." I answered, "Nonsense!" every time and struck
with chains. Weary, weary, I came to the final ocean of acid:
pain was a friend who told me I was temporal when nothing
else spoke, so I dipped in my hand-bones and saw them eaten.

"It is good to be rid of the bones," I felt, "as clattering
encumbrances to search," and dived in whole. However,
instead of being shriven or freed up into flight, oh I
was born again. I squalled for a while to keep my death,

that time when chains were arms and pain a great ally,
but I was conquered and began my sentence to a child's
forgetfulness, uneager to collect the matter of these dreams,
and stared into the present of you innocent beasts.

FUNERAL ORATION FOR A MOUSE

This, Lord, was an anxious brother and
a living diagram of fear: full of health himself,
he brought diseases like a gift
to give his hosts. Masked in a cat's moustache
but sounding like a bird, he was a ghost
of lesser noises and a kitchen pest
for whom some ladies stand on chairs. So,
Lord, accept our felt though minor guilt
for an ignoble foe and ancient sin:
the murder of a guest
who shared our board: just once he ate
too slowly, dying in our trap
from necessary hunger and a broken back.

Humors of love aside, the mousetrap was our own
opinion of the mouse, but for the mouse
it was the tree of knowledge with
its consequential fruit, the true cross
and the gate of hell. Even to approach
it makes him like or better than
its maker: his courage as a spoiler never once
impressed us, but to go out cautiously at night,
into the dining room—what bravery, what
hunger! Younger by far, in dying he
was older than us all: his mobile tail and nose
spasmed in the pinch of our annoyance. Why,
then, at that snapping sound, did we, victorious,
begin to laugh without delight?

Our stomachs, deep in an analysis
of their own stolen baits
(and asking, "Lord, Host, to whom are we the pests?"),
contracted and demanded a retreat
from our machine and its effect of death,
as if the mouse's fingers, skinnier
than hairpins and as breakable as cheese,
could grasp our grasping lives, and in
their drowning movement pull us under too,
into the common death beyond the mousetrap.

I. ENIGMA: CALM: ADDRESSED TO THE AIR

There is the grass to play
with, standing as stiff as nails.

A piece of paper which
was rattled for a week
limps in the lounging air.

Even this breath, all wind
down to the purple lungs
can not blow up a breeze
to clear us out of here.

II. COMMENT ON I.

Here there are armored snails
climbing the grass-blades single file.
Certain as ironclads and as dumb,
they try the heights between
the razor edges of the salt grass
and come a cropper: up
there at the grasses' tips,
swaying in windlessness,
they have to fall. What
will happen to us all
while smothered by the air's
inaction? Slow ourselves,
and waiting for a wind to rise,
we must expect disaster, but
the air is not a savior, iron not
a damned good armor for a fool,

a damned good armor for a fool,
though even love becomes
a doldrum in the tidal
salt-flats of what's beautiful.

HOW WE HEARD THE NAME

The river brought down
dead horses, dead men
and military debris,
indicative of war
or official acts upstream,
but it went by, it all
goes by, that is the thing
about the river. Then
a soldier on a log
went by. He seemed drunk
and we asked him Why
had he and this junk
come down to us so
from the past upstream.
"Friends," he said, "the great
Battle of Granicus
has just been won
by all of the Greeks except
the Lacedaemonians and
myself: this is a joke
between me and a man
named Alexander, whom
all of you ba-bas
will hear of as a god."

MORNING SONG

Look, it's morning, and a little water gurgles in the tap.
I wake up waiting, because it's Sunday, and turn twice more
than usual in bed, before I rise to cereal and comic strips.
I have risen to the morning danger and feel proud,
and after shaving off the night's disguises, after searching
close to the bone for blood, and finding only a little,
I shall walk out bravely into the daily accident.

ORPHEUS

Singing, always singing, he was something
of a prig, like Rilke, and as dangerous
to women. They butchered him; but loud
as ever, wanted or not, the bloody head
continued singing as it drifted out to sea.

Always telling, brave in counsel, ruthlessly glib,
he tamed that barbarous drunk, Dionysus,
out of his ecstasy, and taught the Greeks,
once dirt to the gods and damned to hell,
to pray for heaven, godhood, and himself.

O Maenads, who could choke off his revolt?
Shrined as an oracle, the lovely head
went on with its talking, talking, talking,
until the god, the jealous Apollo himself,
came down in a rage and shut it off.

TRIBUTE TO KAFKA FOR SOMEONE TAKEN

The party is going strong.
The doorbell rings. It's
for someone named me.
I'm coming. I take
a last drink, a last
puff on a cigarette,
a last kiss at a girl,
and step into the hall,
                    bang,
shutting out the laughter. "Is
your name you?" "Yes."
"Well come along then."
"See here. See here. See here."

I will begin again in May, describing weather, how
the wind swept up the dust and pigeons suddenly. Then
the rain began to fall on this and that, the regular
ablutions. The soldiers marched, the cowards wept,
and all were wetted down and winded, crushed.
Soldiers turn the dew to mud. Shivering uncontrollably
because the mild wind blew through wet fatigues,
they fell down in the mud, their pieces fouled,
and groveled in the wilderness, regardless. Some died, and how
I will not tell, since I should speak of weather. Afterwards
the clouds were stripped out of the sky. Palpably fresh,
suckingly sweet like bitten peaches, sparkling like oh,
a peeling tangerine, the air was warmed by light again,
and those who could rise rose like crushed chives from the mud
and stank and thought to dry. The cowards wept
and some got well again, profane with flowers, all was well,
and I have finished now in May. I have described
one circle of a day and those beneath it, but not why.

TRANSCRIBED CONVERSATION IN
PRAISE OF COWS

While it is so that you
can eat a pig from nose
to asshole and beyond,
the cow is usefuller:
the beef, beefsteak, broth,
are healthy, and the milk,
the fine glue from the hooves,
the leather and the horns,
Oh you can take one horn
and blow it and call up
whole armies of believers!

ACTUAL VISION OF MORNING'S EXTRUSION

Gray smoke rose from the morning ground
and separated into spheres. The smoke
or fog of each sphere coiled upon itself
like snakes at love, and hardened into brains:
the corals in the ocean of first light.
These brains grew shells. Mother of pearl, out
clattered the bones! Two ivies intertwined
ran down them searchingly, the red and white
of arteries and nerves, and found their ends.
Nerves hummed in the wind: the running blood,
in pulsing out a heart, induced a warm,
red haze of flesh around a hollow tube,
writhing with appetite, ejection, love,
and hardened in the temperature of dawn.
"Done!" said the clocks, and gave alarm.
Eyes popped into heads as tears amazed.
All hair stood out. All moved and rose
and took a breath: two gasping voids
turned blue with it around the heart.
Shocked into teeth and nails and wrapped
in winding sheets of skin, all souls walked
to test their creatures in their joints,
chinks, and armors as the walking dead,
curious as to what the water, partial sun-light,
ground and mobile air, combined
reactively, could have in mind.

LIFE COMPARISON

Picked up, a hermit crab who seems
to curl up in a dead snail's shell
from cowardice, attacks the thumb
sustaining him in extraordinary air,
regardless, and if he is attacked
by borers or the other enemies of shells,
he crawls out, raw at the rear!,
to find a new place, thus exposed.
So, he does what is appropriate
within his means, within a case,
and fails: oh he could not bite off
the top whorl of my fingerprint,
although he tried. Therefore, I put
him back to sea for courage, for
his doing what he thinks he has to do
while shrinking, and to propitiate
my own incommensurate enemies,
the firms, establishment, and state.

COOLED HEELS LAMENT AGAINST FRIVOLITY, THE MASK OF DESPAIR

Dugan's deathward, darling: you
in your unseeable beauty, oh
fictitious, legal person, need
be only formally concerned,
but there is someone too much here,
perspiring in your waiting room.
Because I did not listen when you said,
"Don't call us: we'll call you,"
your credulous receptionist
believes I am a phony fairy jew
capitalist-communist spy
for Antichrist, a deviated mal-
adjusted lobbyist for the Whiskey Trust,
or else accepts me as I am: a fool.
So while I sit here fouling song,
wasting my substance on the air,
the universe is elsewhere, out
the window in the sky. You,
in your inner office, Muse,
smoking a given, good cigar
and swapping dated stories with
star salesmen of the soul,
refuse to hear my novel pitch
while I sit out here getting old.

ON BEING UNHAPPILY IN LOVE WITH REASON

Rage, closest to reason in the mind,
be cold and smile: you can. The smile of rage
is politic and curls with clarity,
though darker than the black hulk of a tooth,
drumming with ache behind a corner of the lips
that smile to ask the apple-cheek of innocence
up Molars' Alley. So, bite. It snaps against
the pit and hard heart of the ripest fruit
and grows a fast tree barked with pain.
Reason, however, chooses, eats, and spits
external forests for its piece of gain.

So, rage will suffer and do harms,
but may it never be extracted from the face
its beast is manned with: lacking rage,
a mouth falls in upon itself in fear,
the furthest from the reason in the mind,
and sucks its own cheek in to chew
blood's living from the fruits of time.
Reason, closest to rage in the mind,
what can you do but loiter in the mean?,
whose golden apples might offend design
but hang there edibly, while civic teeth
gnash at our only air and latest wild,
and keep their fear of reasoning in mind.

PORTRAIT FROM THE INFANTRY

He smelled bad and was red-eyed with the miseries
of being scared while sleepless when he said
this: "I want a private woman, peace and quiet,
and some green stuff in my pocket. Fuck
the rest." Pity the underwear and socks,
long burnt, of an accomplished murderer,
oh God, of germans and replacements, who
refused three stripes to keep his B.A.R.,
who fought, fought not to fight some days
like any good small businessman of war,
and dug more holes than an outside dog
to modify some Freudian's thesis: "No
man can stand three hundred days
of fear of mutilation and death." What he
theorized was a joke: 'To keep a tight
asshole, dry socks and a you-deep hole
with you at all times." Afterwards,
met in a sports shirt with a round wife, he was
the clean slave of a daughter, a power brake
and beer. To me, he seemed diminished
in his dream, or else enlarged, who knows?,
by its accomplishment: personal life
wrung from mass issues in a bloody time
and lived out hiddenly. Aside from sound
baseball talk, his only interesting remark
was, in pointing to his wife's belly, "If
he comes out left foot first" (the way
you Forward March!), "I am going to stuff
him back up." "Isn't he awful?" she said.

LETTER TO DONALD FALL

I walked a hangover like my death down
the stairs from the shop and opened the door
to a spring snow sticking only to the tops
of air-conditioners and convertibles, and thought
of my friend Donald Fall in San Francisco.
Toothless in spring!, old friend, I count
my other blessings after friendship
unencumbered by communion: I have:
a money-making job, time off it, a wife
I still love sometimes unapproachably
hammering on picture frames, my own
city that I wake to, that the snow
has come to noiselessly at night, it's there
by morning, swallowing the sounds of spring
and traffic, and my new false teeth,
shining and raw in the technician's lab
like Grails, saying, "We are the resurrection
and the life: tear out the green stumps
of your aching and put plastic on instead:
immortality is in science and machines."
I, as an aging phony, stale, woozy, and corrupt
from unattempted dreams and bad health habits,
am comforted: the skunk cabbage generates its
frost-thawing fart-gas in New Jersey and the first
crocuses appear in Rockefeller Center's Channel Gardens:
Fall, it is not so bad at Dugan's Edge.

ON AN ARCHITECT

1

A mine is a hollow tree upside-down in the ground:
the galleries branch out into rooms like leaves
facing and feeding off the rock the way the leaves
exert their palms against the air and drink it.
The tree of earth in the air and its reverse,
the tree of air in the earth, grow up and down
until the word comes: "Put everything back as it was."
Then, after the thundering earthquakes and lightning
of the earth in air, they are no longer there in the same
miraculous silence of their having been there,
except for some hollow and some solid trash
and the metaphysical difference surviving in the image.

2

We poured a pulverized mountain of cement
around an orange-painted mineful of iron
and formed it harder than the term
"concrete" when used in metaphysics to
contrast to "nothing." From the squat
cyclopean basements to the rococco heights
it was a dream. "Fuck 'em all!" I said.
"The janitor can run a jacob's ladder up
the Giants' Staircase and put folding chairs
for hire in the Great Hall: let them pee out
the Rose Window if they have to: there is no
plumbing in my monument." It is; it is
an iron tree, concrete in leaf, meant

to cement man's presence to eternity,
and people pay to enter and be small,
but on these hazy, violet days and with
the sun behind it, oh it seems
almost to disappear, so I went up to it
and hit it. "By my forehead's blood,
oh tricky senses, oh Empirical Philosophers,
I wear the ache that proves it to be there
and not, as light reports, a condensation of the air."

Scoundrels, Scoundrels

ADAM SMITH   KARL MARX

Wheat is
probably
a better
food than
oats,

But if we are to demand that the rate of profit,
say 14.876934.., should be exactly equal in
every business and every year, down to the
hundredth decimal place, on pain of degradation
to a fiction, we should be grossly misunder-
standing the nature of the rate of profit and

but not
than po-
tatoes.

of economic laws in general—none of them has
any reality except as approximation, tendency,
average, but not in *immediate* reality,

Potatoes,
however,
are per-
ishable.

This is partly due to the fact that their action
is thwarted by the simultaneous action of other
laws, but also in part to their own nature as

concepts.

JESUS CHRIST

34. Think not that I
am come to send peace
on earth. I am
not come to send peace,
but a sword.
              35. For I
am come to set a man
at variance against
his father, and
the daughter against
her mother, and
the daughter-in-law against
her mother-in-law.

THESIS, ANTITHESIS, AND NOSTALGIA

Not even dried-up leaves,
skidding like iceboats on
their points down winter streets,
can scratch the surface of
a child's summer and its wealth:
a stagnant calm that seemed
as if it must go on and on
outside of cyclical variety
the way, at child-height on a wall,
a brick named "Ann"
by someone's piece of chalk
still loves the one named "Al"
although the street is vacant and
the writer and the named are gone.

GENERAL PROTHALAMION FOR WARTIMES

Marry. Sweets, tarts and sweets,
come among soots and sherds.
The dairy of the breasts
and warehouse of the balls
will out-last granaries
when grains and futures fall,

granted a lasting. Lust
that lasts a bloodshot night
protected from the air
will breakfast in wrecked day,
excused because it must,
and find its scavenge there.

Given a harvest of wives
and lopping-off of males,
granted that some survive,
the warden of the weak
is number, blood's variety
marauding in the streets.

So, penis, guide the flesh
to shelter in the womb
when sirens and the police
lament all other homes,
and if born, suckling mouths
grow privily with fangs,

well, fangs are promises
to live on what is left,
granted some leavings, and
monsters are replies.
So, marry. Sours and sweets
come among shots and cries.

ON THE ELK, UNWITNESSED

The frantic elk climb from the valleys to escape the flies.
Then, on the heights, they leap, run, and play in snow
as Alces, Alces, glad to be relieved of goads
and ready to get married, due to the wholesome airs.
Those gads downhill, buzzing in armor causative,
must have their joys in cycles too, if the escape
from them in dancing Io!, Io!, on the heights is how,
oh Alces!, Alces!, Hymen triumphs and the roaring stags
fight to assemble harems in the trampled snow
while gad-eggs cradle in their hides and nostrils.

They set out every year diagonally to make
the grand tour of their corner of the world in Oregon,
spurred by a bug at base and climbing up to love
on the apex, and without that lightning touch of Zeus
to slap them, Ha!, Epaphus!, out of the cycling dark
and innocent present of the locally driven beasts,
and toward the widening drive all over Asia and up
into the sky, too, that is the cycle of the really stung.

GRACE FOR THURSDAY

God help us on a day
like this and one of many.
This day was full
of merciful activity
but we got through
at last to supper: lamb
will be good but do
no good: Christ knows
where it will be
tomorrow down the drain.
Oh it was slaughtered like
himself and hung to dry,
so may we eat it up,
talking in mindless ease,
and by the fishwife,
Mary, star of the sea,
ride out the night
and eat some fish on Friday.

STUTTERER

Courage: your tongue has left
its natural position in the cheek
where eddies of the breath
are navigable calms. Now
it locks against the glottis or
is snapped at by the teeth,
in midstream: it must be work
to get out what you mean:
the rapids of the breath
are furious with belief
and want the tongue, as blood
and animal of speech,
to stop it, block it, or come clean
over the rocks of teeth
and down the races of the air,
tumbled and bruised to death.
Relax it into acting, be
the air's straw-hat
canoeist with a mandolin
yodeling over the falls.
This is the sound advice
of experts and a true despair:
it is the toll to pass the locks
down to the old mill stream
where lies of love are fair.

HOLIDAY

After hundreds of years of common sense
action appeared at the corners of all eyes:
lights appeared at night, and sounds of war
whammed from the desert back of town.

At first only the outlying saints saw them,
but later they strolled through the streets:
bat-faced devils walking arm in arm
with blond white angels in a tourists' truce.

It was then that Natural Law was repealed
and a public virgin wept that it was she
to whom a fiend or angel had appeared
announcing an unearthly rape of sorts
and the arrival of a difficult child.

ON THE SUPPOSED IMMORALITY OF ORCHIDS

Orchids are poisonous blooms, though
beautiful, because they flower
rootloose on the air and suck,
instead of solid food,
the vicious disposition of the wind.
Paolo!, Francesca!, with no hope
of hold: take heart in air
as sustenance for flight: plants
can root in the uprooting wind
and take, as rationale,
equivocal beauties from thin air.

Trees get choked by their bouquets
but give support. They praise the bloom.
I damn the means.
Praise teaches. In hunting ways
to root in air but succor hosts,
a moral botanist might find
juster symbiotics on the wind:
plants that will pay, for arboring,
a decorative, fair return,
and trees that will survive
the grapples of the flowers.

MEMORIES OF VERDUN

The men laughed and baaed like sheep
and marched across the flashing day
to the flashing valley. A shaved
pig in a uniform led the way.

I crawled down Old Confusion, hid,
and groaned for years about my crime:
was I the proper coward, they
heroically wrong? I lived out their time!,

a hard labor, convict by look and word:
I was the fool and am penitent:
I was afraid of a nothing, a death;
they were afraid of less, its lieutenant.

WALL, CAVE, AND PILLAR
STATEMENTS, AFTER ASÔKA

In order to perfect all readers
the statements should be carved
on rock walls, on cave walls,
and on the sides of pillars so
the charm of their instruction can
affect the mountain climbers near
the cliffs, the plainsmen near
the pillars, and the city people near
the caves they go to on vacations.

The statements should, and in a fair
script, spell out the right text and gloss
of the Philosopher's jocular remark. Text:
"Honesty is the best policy." Gloss:
"He means not 'best' but 'policy,'
(this is the joke of it) whereas in fact
      Honesty is Honesty, Best
      is Best, and Policy is Policy,
      the three terms being not
      related, but here loosely allied.
What is more important is that 'is'
is, but the rocklike truth of the text
resides in the 'the'. The 'the' is The.
      By this means the amusing sage
      has raised or caused to be raised
      the triple standard in stone:
the single is too simple for life,
the double is mere degrading hypocrisy,
but the third combines the first two
in a possible way, and contributes

something unsayable of its own:
this is the pit, nut, seed, or stone
of the fruit when the fruit has been
digested:

It is good to do good for the wrong
reason, better to do good for the good
reason, and best of all to do good
good: i.e. when the doer and doee
and whatever passes between them
are beyond all words like 'grace'
or 'anagogic insight,' or definitions like
'particular instance of a hoped-at-law,'
and which the rocks alone can convey.
This is the real reason for the rock walls,
the cave walls and pillars, and not the base
desires for permanence and display
that the teacher's conceit suggests."

That is the end of the statements, but,
in order to go on a way after the end
so as to make up for having begun
after the beginning, and thus to come around
to it in order to include the whole thing,
add: "In some places the poignant slogan,
'Morality is a bad joke like everything else,'
may be written or not, granted that space
exists for the vulgar remarks, the dates,
initials and hearts of lovers, and all
other graffiti of the prisoners of this world."

POEMS TWO

(1963)

THREE AS A MAGIC NUMBER

Three times dark, first in the mind,
second in January, the pit of the year,
and third in subways going up and down
the hills and valleys underground,
I go from indoors to indoors indoors,
seeing the Hudson River three times a week
from my analyst's penthouse window. It
is a brilliant enlargement three ways:
in and out and fluvial. The river goes
like white smoke from the industries
to the north, and the rigged-up lights
of the Palisades Amusement Park
promise a west of pleasure, open space,
and a circus of whippable lions,
while the cliffs beneath them, made
of latent vegetation, the live rock,
and a fall of snow, seems to me to be
the hanging gardens of Hammurabi.

ROMANCE OF THE ESCAPED CHILDREN

Goodbye, children: the bad Good Knight
is through. The rescued girl is asleep,
dreaming of ransom and astrologers
in the highest room of the family Keep.

On the second floor the Him Himself
is sound asleep among his pudding wife
and in the great Ground Hall below
retainers denounce the family wine

and pick at the bones of a cold dwarf.
Down in the cellars you shivered about,
continuous shrieks applaud the rack: he is,
from top to bottom, a good to bad scout,

domestic in the middle. You are fortunate
to have escaped from this on muffled oars.

COAT OF ARMS

In memory of E. A. Dugan

My father's Memory Book
was warm before the womb
among gymnasium smells
of resolutions put to dust.
The grand tour of his squint
that stopped for photographs
before each sepia Wonder
found Ithaca and ease
beneath the attic dust.
What a joker, like me:
he came into the womb
where I was, poked around
and spat and left and I
was forced out wet
into the cold air. Someone
slapped me and I wept
to have become a traveling man.
Oh I inherited his book
stamped with a coat of arms
self-made from dreams—
a moon and family beast,
a phrase around a shield
boldly nicked with feats
and warm before the womb—
and wondered, laughing, why,
when heroes have come home
from labors out of time
they loll out fatherhood
in baseball-worship, old

underclothes, odd sales jobs
and bad stories often told,
told often, stories often told,
but in one photograph,
the last before the womb,
the dragon had been stuffed
and shipped off home,
authentically killed, and he
is posed in mail, his head
fixed in a photographer's clamp
and Coney Island smile
graced by the cry: "INHIBIT!"
So I learned to rent arms too,
and go out broke without
escutcheon, with a blank
shield against all critics and
a motto of my own
devising on the rim:

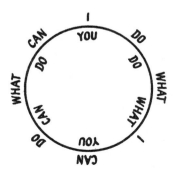

and throw down a left-handed glove
under the cry: "ETCETERA!"

ELEGY

I know but will not tell
you, Aunt Irene, why there
are soapsuds in the whiskey:
Uncle Robert had to have
a drink while shaving. May
there be no bloodshed in your house
this morning of my father's death
and no unkept appearance
in the living, since he has
to wear the rouge and lipstick
of your ceremony, mother,
for the first and last time:
father, hello and goodbye.

TWO QUITS AND A DRUM,
AND ELEGY FOR DRINKERS

1. ON ASPHALT: NO GREENS

Quarry out the stone
of land, cobble the beach,
wall surf, name it "street,"
allow no ground or green
cover for animal sins,
but let opacity of sand
be glass to keep the heat
outside, the senses in.
Then, when time's Drunk,
reeling to death, provokes
god's favor as a fool,
oh let a lamp post grow
out of its absence, bend,
heavy with care, and bloom
light. Let a curb extrude
a comfortable fault. Let
"street" become a living room.
Comfortably seated, lit
by the solicitude of "lamp,"
the Drunk and street are one.
They say, "Let's have no dirt:
bulldoze the hills into
their valleys: make it plain.
Then take the mountains down
and let their decks of slate
be dealt out flat grey.
Let their mating seams
be tarred against the weeds

by asphalt, by the night's
elixir of volcanoes hotly poured."
Then the soulless port at night
is made a human, and the Drunk
god: no one else is here
to be so but who cares?

2. PORTRAIT AGAINST WOMEN

Bones, in his falling,
must have hit the skin
between themselves and stone,
but distances of wine
were his upholstery
against the painful crime
of lying in the street,
since "God protects them."
He rolled onto his back,
his right hand in his fly,
and gargled open-mouthed,
showing the white of an eye:
it did not see the sign
raised on the proper air
that read: "Here lies
a god-damned fool. Beware."
No: his hand, his woman, on
the dry root of his sex,
debates it: deformed by wine
and fantasy, the wreck

of infant memory is there,
of how the garden gate
slammed at the words, "Get
out you god-damned bum,"
and so he was, since she,
goddess, mother, and wife,
spoke and it was the fact.
Her living hair came out
gray in his hand, her teeth
went false at his kiss,
and her solid flesh went slack
like mother's. "Now, lady, I
am sick and out of socks,
so save me: I am pure although
my hand is on my cock."
Then he could rise up young
out of his vagrancy
in whole unwilled reform
and shuck the fallen one,
his furlough in this street
redeemed by her grace.
There would be the grass
to lay her on, the quench
of milk behind the taste of wine,
and laughter in a dreamed
jungle of love behind
a billboard that could read:
"This is YOUR Garden:
Please keep it clean."

3. COURAGE. EXCEED.

A beggar with no legs below
the middle of his knees
walked down Third Avenue
on padded sockets, on
his telescoped or
anti-stilted legs
repeating, "Oh beautiful
faspacious skies!" upon
a one-man band: a bass
drum on roller-skates,
a mouth-high bugle clamped
to it, and cymbals interlocked
inside a fate of noise. He
flew the American flag
for children on a stick
stuck in a veteran's hat,
and offered pencils. He
was made of drunks' red eyes.
He cried, "Courage! Exceed!"
He was collapsed in whole
display. Drunkards, for this
and with his pencil I
put down his words drunk:
"Stand! Improvise!"

4. ELEGY FOR DRINKERS

What happened to the drunks
I used to know, the prodigals
who tried their parents' help
too far? Some misers of health
have aged out dry; the rest
are sick and out of socks,
their skin-tight anklebones
blue as the mussel shells
that rolled in Naxos' surf
when Bacchus danced ashore
and kicked them all to hell.

> Oh gutter urinal,
> be Dirce's holy stream,
> so lightning out of Zeus
> can rage on Semele,
> invited! Permit her son,
> issuant of His thigh,
> to rule her family
> as Bromios, god of wine!

Oh Dionisos, good god
of memory and sleep,
you grace the paper bag,
stuck in the fork of a crutch,
that holds the secret sons
and furniture of bums,
since wine is the cure of wine.

It's thanks to you that I,
in my condition, am
still possible and praising: I
am drunk today, but what
about tomorrow? I burnt
my liver to you for a drink,
so pay me for my praises:
for thirty-seven cents, for
the price of a pint of lees,
I would praise wine, your name,
and how your trouble came
out of the east to Thebes:
you taught the women wine
and tricked King Pentheus
to mask as one of them:
because his father died
to all appeals for help,
the rending penalty,
death at his mother's hands!,
still fills The Bowery
with prodigals of hope:
they pray for lightning and
a dance to their god damn,
since wine is the cure of wine
and wine the cure wine cured
and wine the cure of wine.

TO A RED-HEADED DO-GOOD WAITRESS

Every morning I went to her charity and learned
to face the music of her white smile so well
that it infected my black teeth as I escaped,
and those who saw me smiled too and went in
the White Castle, where she is the inviolable lady.

There cripples must be bright, and starvers noble:
no tears, no stomach-cries, but pain made art
to move her powerful red pity toward philanthropy.
So I must wear my objectively stinking poverty
like a millionaire clown's rags and sing, "Oh I

got plenty o' nuttin'," as if I made
a hundred grand a year like Gershwin, while
I get a breakfast every day from her for two
weeks and nothing else but truth: she has
a policeman and a wrong sonnet in fifteen lines.

ON A SEVEN-DAY DIARY

Oh I got up and went to work
and worked and came back home
and ate and talked and went to sleep.
Then I got up and went to work
and worked and came back home
from work and ate and slept.
Then I got up and went to work
and worked and came back home
and ate and watched a show and slept.
Then I got up and went to work
and worked and came back home
and ate steak and went to sleep.
Then I got up and went to work
and worked and came back home
and ate and fucked and went to sleep.
Then it was Saturday, Saturday, Saturday!
Love must be the reason for the week!
We went shopping! I saw clouds!
The children explained everything!
I could talk about the main thing!
What did I drink on Saturday night
that lost the first, best half of Sunday?
The last half wasn't worth this "word."
Then I got up and went to work
and worked and came back home
from work and ate and went to sleep,
refreshed but tired by the weekend.

CREDO

They told me, "You don't have
    to work: you can starve,"
so I walked off my job
    and went broke. All day
I looked for love and cash
    in the gutters and found
a pencil, paper, and a dime
    shining in the fading light,
so I ate, drank, and wrote:
    "It is no use: poverty
is worse than work, so why
    starve at liberty? when I
can eat as a slave, drink
    in the evening, and pay
for your free love at night."

ELEGY FOR A GIFTED CHILD

Ephemeron! It's over! All
the scales of the clock-faces
are so heavy with life,
so loaded to capacity
with eyelids and lashes,
that they have come around again
to zero, midnight. Since you
were no Faust at noon,
no Mephistopheles at midnight
will reward your prayers with Hell
and its continuous distractions: it's
just all over, Ephemeron.

COUNTER-ELEGY

Oh no. I go on
doing what I have
to do because I do
it: I sat and sat
there counting one
plus one plus one
while all the rest
were somewhere else,
playing in the tripe
of a living horse
and stroking its great
eyes: this took time!
Then at the end
of that eternity
they gave me 60 bucks

less taxes and dues
and said, "Come back
tomorrow; there
is always work to do."
It was night! I went out!
Oh I got stewed,
screwed and tattooed!
My skin read: I LOVE
MY MOTHER in a heart
pierced by a naked sword!
Weak in the needling, it
was there for all life long
in the bent branch of my arm.
You think I just
went off like a bomb
and was over, but
it has seemed long to me,
slow as the explosion of
the whole life of the tree
in which the birds evolved,
each singing out its song.

WINTER'S ONSET FROM
AN ALIENATED POINT OF VIEW

The first cold front came in
whining like a carpenter's plane
and curled the warm air
up the sky: winter is
for busy work, summer
for construction. As for
spring and fall, ah, you
know what we do then:
sow and reap. I want
never to be idle or by plumb
or level to fear death,
so I do none of this
in offices away from weather.

ON HAT: ON VERTICAL MOBILITY
AS A CONCEPT

From the official hurry on the top floor
and through the irony on the working floors
down to the sleep stolen in the basement,
the company went on incorporate and firm,
drumming like an engine through the spring day.
Standing still but often going up and down
while breaking in a new winter felt hat,
the elevator operator was the best man in
the place in humor. Going from the thieves
at the top to the bums in the cellar
and past the tame working people in between,
he was denoting Plato's ideal form of Hat
vertically in an unjust state in the spring:
he did nothing but social service for nothing
as a form to be walked on like stairs.

The receptionist has shiny fingernails
since she has buffed them up for hours,
not for profit but for art, while they,
the partners, have been arguing themselves
the further into ruthless paranoia,
the accountant said. The sales representatives
came out against the mustard yellow: "It
looks like baby-shit," and won, as ever. In
the studio, the artist, art director, and
the copy chief were wondering out loud:
Whether a "Peace On Earth" or a "Love
And Peace On Earth" should go around
the trumpeting angel on the Christmas card.
In this way the greeting card company
worked back and forth across a first spring
afternoon like a ferryboat on the river:
time was passing, it itself was staying the same,
and workers rode it on the running depths
while going nowhere back and forth across
the surface of the river. Profits flow away
in this game, and thank god there is none
of the transcendence printed on the product.

FREE VARIATION ON A
TRANSLATION FROM GREEK

In times of peace and good government
there is increase of fruits and ease.
The house-spider tries to spin her web
from the air raid helmet to the gun
in the closet, but quits at the sound
of the morning vacuum cleaner: the sound
father keeps his weapons clean but locked away.
The afternoon is broad. The evening
is for supper and nothing. At night the ex-
soldier can wake from honey-hearted sleep
and turn to his own wife in his own
bed for a change, for solace against fears
of death by normal attrition. At 6 A.M.
there are no police knocking: his only problems,
besides the major ones of love, work, and death,
are noisy children: playing out in the street
before breakfast and against his rules, a joke
occurs, and their laughter starts, builds,
and then goes up like a prayer against the rules
and for the time of peace and good government
in which it happens: they could have lit
a used Christmas tree: it goes up in fire
but burns invisibly in the clear morning air
while roaring. Then he goes to work again,
instead of war, and the day stands as said.

THE REPEALER: "YOU'RE TOO WILD"

You laughed with an open mouth
to show the flowering ivory
of your temporary teeth because
you hit him on the head hard
with a croquet mallet, drawing
real blood. Now I know you as
the laugher and the hammerer,
as Charles Martel The Churl
who comes to change the past
with blood and laughter. Don't
fall to the grief that makes
your father beat you up, but
encourage your essence! Be-
jewel your mallet and strike
for a world of growing joy.

ON GOING LATENT

Arcadia was square and fenced
with upright planks. It had
a slate path pretended as
a stream of square meander
which I hopped and helped
my mother May to cross.
Roses were tied to sticks
in dirty holes in the grass.
Once I saw a snake
and ran away indoors,
crying of hell, and stopped
her conversation with an aunt.
Armored in women, I
returned and found the worm
groveling in laughter: it
had crucified the roses and
had made a fool of snakes
before I did or did not
stamp it out. I fell asleep
and did not wake up later,
until I woke up far away
and worked to be your lover.

FOR MASTURBATION

I have allowed myself
this corner and am God.
Here in the must
beneath their stoop
I will do as I will,
either as act as act,
or dream for the sake of dreams,
and if they find me out
in rocket ships or jets
working to get away,

then let my left great-toe-
nail grow into the inside knob
of my right ankle bone and let
my fingernails make eight new moons
temporarily in the cold salt marches of my palms!
THIS IS THE WAY IT IS, and if
it is "a terrible disgrace"
it is as I must will,
because I am not them
though I am theirs to kill.

ON BREEDING, FROM PLUTARCH

After the victory he loped
through town, still bloodily
unwounded, grinning like a dog
aroused, and with his sword
hanging down from his hand.
The Spartans yelled, "Go screw
What's-her-name just as you are,
crazy and stinking with war!
Her husband will be proud,
or say he is, when she,
yielding, conceives a noble child."

Confusedly, I used to think
of the wind as the item
connoting evanescence, and of stone
as the permanent thing, but
stone is blown full of holes
by the wind. The fighters' toes
in the Halicarnassus frieze
are corrupt with the athlete's foot
of many years of endurance,
or with some other wasting power.
Elgin! Where are the penises
and noses? A Captain Hammond
took two heads to Denmark;
other heads cut in half
show how the stone's brains
are full of incidents. Who cares
whether the faces are chopped off
or not? The fine grains of the stone
in the inside of their heads
are full of reasonable patterns.
The stone thought of the stone
figures is thus exposed:

       that the marble is
       processional like its friezes
       of gods, people, and beasts
       and their grasses fed by water
       down from the rock tables
       in the mountains where
       the marbles came from in

their process from the quarry
to the dust motes in a sunbeam
entering a dead museum
and goes off someplace else
I can not know about while going.

POEM

Whatever was living is dead
and a lot of what was dead
has begun to move around,
so who knows what
the plan for a good state
is: they all go out
on the roads! Wherever
they came from is down,
wherever they're going
is not up yet, and everything
must make way, so,
now is the time to plan
for a new city of man.
The sky at the road's end
where the road goes up
between one hill and ends,
is as blank as my mind,
but the cars fall off
into great plains beyond,
so who knows what
the plan for a good state
is: food, fuel, and rest
are the services, home
is in travel itself,
and burning signs at night
say DYNAFLO! to love,
so everything goes.

ON AN ACCIDENT:
ON A NEWSPAPER STORY

When a child turned in a false
alarm, a deaf man walked in front
of the fire engine. The attraction
between deafness and clangor is so
powerful, and some drivers are so
Christ-like—in saving the one
they damage many—that ten
people went to Coney Island Hospital
to lie as culls of the event among
the other victims of the Whip,
the Cyclone, and the Tunnel of Love.
Children can act largely, death
can be small, and art can go on
from the pains of its individuals.

851

A flying pigeon hit me on a fall day
because an old clothes buyer's junk cart
had surprised it in the gutter: license 851.
The summer slacks and skirts in the heap
looked not empty and not full of their legs,
and a baseball cap remained in head-shape.
Death is a complete collector of antiques
who finds, takes, and bales each individual
of every species all the time for sale to god,
and I, too, now have been brushed by wings.

FABRICATION OF ANCESTORS

For old Billy Dugan, shot in the ass in the Civil War,
my father said.

The old wound in my ass
has opened up again, but I
am past the prodigies
of youth's campaigns, and weep
where I used to laugh
in war's red humors, half
in love with silly-assed pains
and half not feeling them.
I have to sit up with
an indoor unsittable itch
before I go down late
and weeping to the storm-
cellar on a dirty night
and go to bed with the worms.
So pull the dirt up over me
and make a family joke
for Old Billy Blue Balls,
the oldest private in the world
with two ass-holes and no
place more to go to for a laugh
except the last one. Say:
The North won the Civil War
without much help from me
although I wear a proof
of the war's obscenity.

AUTUMN AT BAIAE: FOR CAVAFY

The women, clients, and slaves wept
and pretended the louder as he read
the temporal restitution of his thefts,
but the men stared: panic and avarice
exploded behind their eyes, shaded
from the candidate for certain lightning.
"Now, being condemned to a glory I
can neither avoid nor survive, I make
my will." Then, like a combat officer
committed for the last time to the point
of fire, M. C. Tacitus drove away
for his two hundred days as Emperor.

POEM

In the old days either the plaintiff or the defendant won or lost
justly or unjustly according to the mood of the court; the innocent
and the guilty were acquitted or condemned according to their luck
or pull with justice. Nowadays they are all condemned to death
by hard labor, together with the lawyers, juries, and arresting police.
Then the boards of review condemn the presiding judges, too,
for having wasted time. In this way, all those who are in any way
connected with justice are impartially disconnected, and the clerk
closes the court house to join the last judgement. This is not to say
that there is no more justice: as an only natural human invention to
begin with, it has turned into the needs of the state, which needs labor.
The whole apparatus can be forgotten in the absence of individuals
to whom to apply it, and the sensible man will have nothing to do
with anything outside his inner, passional life except his position.

RIDING SONG FOR A SEMI-FEUDAL ARMY,
FOR GLUBB PASHA,
FOR TORTURED COLONELS

On a brilliant morning in May
we stole horses and set out
after the enemy (six kibbutzniks
gossiping about their tractors,
tractors and trivia), tired as usual
and dirty, but laughing and talking
of love. Then the poet of the left
flushed a quail, shot it through the eye,
jumped a rock pile, caught it
as it fell, and gave it to the Colonel, saying:

"On a brilliant morning in May
we stole horses and set out
after the enemy (six kibbutzniks
debating the yokelization
of the intelligentsia). We were dirty and tired
as usual, but we laughed and talked
dirtily of love. Then I shot
a bird in the eye, caught it as it fell
so as to save the flesh intact
and gave it to the Colonel, saying:

'Who knows who will be alive
tomorrow? In the meantime I will give
the Colonel the bird to make him
able in strategy, careful in tactics, and
respectful of these lives of ours,
not that they matter: he
deserves a good last supper tonight.' "

The Colonel accepted the gift, laughing,
and turned to the war correspondent
riding beside him and said, "Now

you see why I like to sneak out
of the office and ride with these kids."
"I see," said the reporter. "It is vanity."
"The Colonel got the bird," said the poet.
"And we rode on after the enemy (six
kibbutzniks debating Martin Buber's so-called position),
fooling away our fear and dreaming
of peace and glory at the same time,
which is impossible, though death is not:
the Israelis are anti-romantic."

ON LINES 69-70, BOOK IV,
OF VIRGIL'S *AENEID*

Aeneas: *Then I will found a temple of solid marble to*
Phoebus and Trivia.

You can read the pictures stamped
on the brass door: there
is Aeneas in chin and black boots
doing the Roman salute
as Dido tears at her hair.
The curly waves of the sea
perform close-order drill
while the purple corpse of Pan
disorders the public air
to show that Christ is here.
Long bugles of government
blow to their hearts' content
that honor is murderous.
I even saw Orpheus
sailing in Jason's fleet
and plucking a civic lyre
in praise of colonial fleece.
"That's enough," the priestess said.
"You came here in holy dread
and do not have the time
to laugh at the art any more.
I enlist whatever is mine,
so come in and fill out the forms."

GENERAL PROTHALAMION
IN POPULOUS TIMES

Air is the first international
when soldiers smell the girls
and funerals in flowers in
contained wars in spring. They swear
allegiance to the air and are
remobilized for the campaigns
of love nightly, in sexual cells,
subverted by the nose to be
patriots of what is not
or partisans of a rose,
but go on drilling. So, fall out
on sick call for a shot
against the air and go on
killing. A private Eden blooms
like a grenade inside their skulls,
corporal with apples, snakes, and Eves,
exploding outward toward the fall
from summer's marching innocence
to the last winter of general war.

ADMONITOR: A PEARL FOR ARROGANCE

In winter a crow flew at my head
because her fledgling warmed
the brute nest of my fist. Ah,
the pearl clipped in her yellow beak
fell from her cry of "Ransom," and
I freed my bird for grace.

There in the pearl I prophesied
a ball to gaze in, with the stars
mirrored upon it as it held
the image of the crow at core.
Spread-eagled in the royal orb,
the black bird grew, one foot
holding lightning and the other,
worms: a herald arrogance.
I saw my fortune, iridescent
with deceit, my golden mask
the operative profile on a coin
haloed in motto: Order Reigns,
and backed by pestilent wings.

The window in this easter egg
exposed the blood's close tenement
where out-sized eyes, two bright
black pebbles in tarred grass,
were imminent with birth,
and hunger's instrument, the beak,
armored its hinterland of flesh
with bone. It will crack out
of art, the image at full term,
and cast about for meal.

How I hoped for a peaceable bird,
foolish as the gooney or dove!,
that would crack out of will
unhungry but immune to fists,
but I expect some arrogance
in flesh, be it of pigeons
or flightless birds, and do not know
a trustable source of order in
designs. I hear of Yeats' trick,
autocratic in the metal,
and of Picasso's normative dove,
gala with hopes, but what I eat
is this admonitory crow.

THE CRIMES OF BERNARD

They were always arguing that we
were either the Devil's puppets or
God's marionettes, so when I said,
"What's the difference?, the latter
has us by the long hairs, the former
by the short, the best thing
about Commedia dell'Arte is
improvisation," they said, 'There
are only two sides to a question: to
propose a third is treason if true.
Traitors we snatch bald, we
cut off their bells, we set them out
naked on the road to nowheres
as two-bit Abélards, two-bit whores,
and go on arguing as before."

ON VISITING CENTRAL PARK ZOO

The animals, hanging around in forms,
are each resigned to be what each one is,
imprisoned twice, in flesh first, then in irons.
The Bactrian camel is adjusted or is not
as, with his humps collapsed for lack of need
for water and with useless tufts of hair
like hummocks on the great plains of his flanks,
he stands around in shape and chews
a curd of solace, whether bitter, bland, or sweet,
who knows? Such is his formal pride,
his gargoyle's face remains a stone
assertion as he pisses in between his splayed,
seemingly rachitic legs and stays
that way, in place, for want of something else
to do, caught in his double prison all the time.
Whatever he is, he goes on being what he is,
although ridiculous in forced review,
perseverant in not doing what he need not do.

THE LIFE AND DEATH
OF THE CANTATA SYSTEM

When the Lord was a man of war and sailed out
through the sky at night with all the stars
of all the constellations as his riding lights,
those beneath his oceanic, personal ascendancy
ascended in fated systems. The massed shouts
of the chorus sailed a regular sea of violins
as Galleons of the Line!, with hulls of bassos,
decks of baritones and altos, ornate in poop
and prow in rigging up the masts of soloists
which bore aloft, in turn, soprano mainsails,
topgallants of the children's chorus, and
pennants of castrati streaming on the heights!
The Great Armada sang "Invincible!" to the deep,
but when the time came for a change in craft
the Lord's storms wrecked the vessels of the Lord
and the voices poured out on the air still singing.
The Empirical English conquered in the shallows. He
withdrew his stars to favor those made by machines.

PLAGUE OF DEAD SHARKS

Who knows whether the sea heals or corrodes?
The wading, wintered pack-beasts of the feet
slough off, in spring, the dead rind of the shoes'
leather detention, the big toe's yellow horn
shines with a natural polish, and the whole
person seems to profit. The opposite appears
when dead sharks wash up along the beach
for no known reason. What is more built
for winning than the swept-back teeth,
water-finished fins, and pure bad eyes
these old, efficient forms of appetite
are dressed in? Yet it looks as if the sea
digested what it wished of them with viral ease
and threw up what was left to stink and dry.
If this shows how the sea approaches life
in its propensity to feed as animal entire,
then sharks are comforts, feet are terrified,
but they vacation in the mystery and why not?
Who knows whether the sea heals or corrodes?:
what the sun burns up of it, the moon puts back.

FROM HERACLITUS

Matter is palsy: the land heaving, water
breaking against it, the planet whirling
days in night. Even at the still point
of night I hear the jockeying for place
of each thing wrestling with itself
to be a wrestler. Is the stress that holds
them, whirling in themselves, an ache?
If so strained to shape and aching for release,
explode to peace! But I am here poised
within this eddy, sentenced to a shape,
and have to wrestle through a gust of violence
before I sleep; so may I make or augment
all these lights at night, so as to give out
all the temporary ornaments I can to peace.

ON FINDING THE
MEANING OF "RADIANCE"

The dreamed Grail found as if in dreams
was not as had been dreamed when found.
The blasted pot, so early in the earth
that it was nearly dirt in dirt, was fired
either in a kiln or a volcano: who can tell
a thumb or tool mark from an earthquake's
pressure in time, and what's the difference?
It is all part of the same process. In
the crater of the natural or potter's pot
there still is some of the first fluid.
It is, and why not say it, Perceval?,
pisslike, with a float of shit on top,
body and blood having changed in time
to what the beasts give back to the ground
with their personalities. Once drained,
the treasure is there in the lees, changed.
The gold filigree, once dreamed to be
a fine vein in the ore with the ore removed,
has run back into its rock, and the gems,
chipped facet by facet from their shells,
are back fast in their stones again, asleep;
but the gold lightning and jewels of fire
are freed in the finding of them, freed
by the nauseous draught: the fire balled
in the skull, the lightning veining the veins.
So I am freed to say, as a piece of dirt
to the body of earth: "Here is where love is,"
and, "This is the meaning of 'Radiance.'"

113

A GIFTS ACCOMPANIMENT

The central stone is small, small,
refractive, faceted, and red,
but small because of costs;
oh I can give no larger. Be
distracted from the jewel
which is so small by all
the craft of filigree around it:
it has been worked: it holds
a one night's curiosity
of intertwining stems and leaves,
radiant in ivy from the stone
which is so small. Look at
its corolla: the silvered multiple
details, man-houred craftily
around that stone, are by
love's labors a disguise
of poverty's small heart
in hopes the saying is a lie
that says: "Small hearts evoke
small fates and no delights."
See how the spider-legged clasp
is soldered practically in back
so you (if you accept it though
the stone, expense, and heart
are small because of costs)
could wear it on the dress
you wear around the chest
you wear around your heart.
Please be the setting of
the setting of the setting of
this heart which is so small
though I can give no larger.

ARGUMENT TO LOVE AS A PERSON

The cut rhododendron branches
flowered in our sunless flat.
Don't complain to me, dear,
that I waste your life in poverty:
you and the cuttings prove: Those
that have it in them to be beautiful
flower wherever they are!, although
they are, like everything else, ephemeral.
Freedom is as mortal as tyranny.

WHAT THE HELL, RAGE,
GIVE IN TO NATURAL GRACES

She walks. This never has
been done before. She knows
how it is done: her forearms
raised, waving her hands
on the natural rachets of her wrists,
she takes steps! She balances
on black spike heels so sharp
that they would pierce your heart
if she could walk on you,
and smiles to show it off:
this is a giddy new art
she owns squealing because
she steps on certain things—
spittle and cigarette butts
littered from some past—
and comes back from the store
with the first ice-cream cone
in the whole world to date,
her walking being as light
as my irony is heavy.
She blinks rapidly when
she tells me all this because
wild insects of perception get
into her eyes and bite them.
Thinking of history, oh I
must speak of What's-her-name,
sweet sixteen and never been
and never will be, just is;
but speak of love and she's
a sweet one to the senses,

palpably adequate, e-
motionally to be husbanded
because the world is weird
because it's here while she
is. Yesterday would surprise
her if she heard of it,
as will tomorrow when she does,
or else not. As of now,
things are for the first
and last time timeless like
the Classic Comic strips
and known to her agreeably
except for stepped-on things
littered from some past,
so what the hell, rage,
give in to native graces:
her brains are in her tits!,
as she knows bouncingly,
and there for all to love,
since the world fights its war
in her womb and so far wins.

A SAWYER'S RAGE AGAINST
TREES NOBLE AS HORSES

1.

Inwardly centered like a child
sucking soda through a straw,
they have their noses in the dirt,
greedily absent, blinded, while
their green behinds in the wind
wave back and forth. Oh I can
hit them and they won't hit back.
Oh let them all come down, slow-
ly at the first inclination from
the vertical, then faster, then
crashing in passion! There is
a hallelujah from the dust and birds,
and insects are set free of hell
in devilish shapes to shrivel in
the solid glare of the day, fools
to the contrary, who maintain
that Christ is down from the heights
by this, to the mother earth again.

2.

It is even, the way the trees,
in coming up from the ground,
from nothing, from a nut,
take liberties in spreading out
like animals, like us. But, brutes
of a chosen ground, they stand
around in suction, dark, grouped

like witnesses afraid to act
beside the accidents of roads
and more afraid to cross except
packed in a squirrel's cheek,
in nuts, or in a fairy's flight
of seed. Their undersides are dark
in contrast to the strong, blond,
human inner arm; even the ground
beneath them is a hairy damp,
dirty as groins. Oh we will cut
them down to boards, pulp, dust,
and size: fury the ax, fury the saw
will cure their spreading stands;
courage will make the world plain.

IN THE FOREST

it was warm and cold,
cold from the damps because
it all took place in trees.
When it rained it rained
and when the rain stopped
the trees rained in the wind
and when the trees stopped
it rained. So it went.

Once it was huddling, once
it was sitting apart, once
it was bleeding in time.
We ate and we drank
and we slept and we
did something else
we should not talk about.
Was it love? It was all
supposed to be love.

My it was dark
at night. Whoever it was
who planned that place
forgot the lighting
although some claim to see.

ON TREES

Secular Metamorphosis of
Joyce Kilmer's "Trees"

Don't talk to me about trees having branches and roots:
they are all root, except for the trunk, and the high root,
waving its colors in the air, is no less snarled in its food
than is the low root snarled in its specialty: nourishment
in dirt. What with the reciprocal fair trade of the trunk
holding the two roots together and apart in equipoise,
the whole tree stands in solid connection to its whole self
except for the expendable beauty of its seasonal ends,
and is so snarled at either end in its contrary goods
that it studs the dirt to the air with its living wood.
This anagogic significance grows with its growth for years,
twigging in all directions as an evidence of entirety,
although it waves back and forth in the wind and is a host
to fungi, insects, men, birds, and the law of entropy.

POEM

What was once an island with birds,
palms, snakes, and goats in flowers
is now a sand-bar bearing sea clams.
A storm at sea washed over it and it
drowned. There is no food but what
the surf throws up to it and no sweet
water but what the sky throws down.
You are cast away one storm too late
to know the previous ecology,
so may you leave it soon, or fertilize
the sand-bar for another kind of life:
you can do nothing except your part
unless you want a short survival badly.
So what if you act like a storm against
sweet water, other castaways, and clams?
They will give out!, as you will, soon:
no more interrelational elegance
will burgeon on this desert in the sea,
and no prayers make it bear analogies.

MONOLOGUE OF A
COMMERCIAL FISHERMAN

"If you work a body of water and a body of woman
you can take fish out of one and children out of the other
for the two kinds of survival. The fishing is good,
both kinds are adequate in pleasures and yield,
but the hard work and the miseries are killing;
it is a good life if life is good. If not, not.
You are out in the world and in in the world,
having it both ways: it is sportive and prevenient living
combined, although you have to think about the weathers
and the hard work and the miseries are what I said.
It runs on like water, quickly, under the boat,
then slowly like the sand dunes under the house.
You survive by yourself by the one fish for a while
and then by the other afterward when you run out.
You run out a hooky life baited with good times,
and whether the catch is caught or not is a question
for those who go fishing for men or among them for things."

VARIATION ON A
THEME BY STEVENS

In fall and whiskey weather when
the eye clears with the air and blood
comes up to surface one last time
before the winter and its sleeps,
the weeds go down to straws,
the north wind strips most birds
out of the atmosphere and they
go southward with the sunlight,
the retired people, and rich airs.
All appetites revive and love
is possible again in clarity
without the sweats of heat: it makes
warmth. The walleyed arctic birds
arrive to summer in the fall,
warmed by these chills; geese
practice their noisy Vs,
half a horizon wide, and white owls
hide from their crows in the pines.
Therefore it is not tragic to stay
and not tragic or comic to go,
but it is absolutely typical to say
goodbye while saying hello.

FROM ROME. FOR MORE PUBLIC
FOUNTAINS IN NEW YORK CITY

Oh effervescent palisades of ferns in drippage,
the air sounds green by civic watered bronze
fountains in New York City. Hierarchs of spray
go up and down in office: they scour the noons
when hot air stinks to itself from Jersey's smoke
and the city makes itself a desert of cement.
Moses! Command the sun to august temperance!
When water rises freely over force and poises,
cleaning itself in the dirty air, it falls back
on the dolphins, Poseidon, and moss-headed nymphs,
clean with the dirt of air left cleansed by its
clear falling, and runs down coolly with the heat
to its commune, pooling. What public utility!
The city that has working fountains, that lights
them up at night electrically, that does not say
to thirsters at its fountains: DO NOT DRINK!—
that city is well ordered in its waters and drains
and dresses its corruption up in rainbows, false
to the eye but how expressive of a cool truth being.
The unitary water separates, novel on its heights,
and falls back to its unity, discoursing. So let
New York City fountains be the archives of ascent
that teach the low high styles in the open air
and frondage of event! Then all our subway selves
could learn to fall with grace, after sparkling,
and the city's life acknowledge the water of life.

ACCOMMODATION TO DETROIT

"When good people die they become worms in Detroit," they say.
"When bad people die they go to Hamtramck just as they are."
It is all right to mock it, but some are exalted: they
have escaped to the cities from the badlands to the south
and see them as their Edens found, with Eves and the fruits
and shelter under iron trees. They have had a hard life
as draught animals, and are here to try out human life,
temptations first. They are walled away from their wilderness
by absence in stone and iron, the way Hamtramck is walled
by Detroit, city in city, cement in cement, and seed in shell.
Greater Detroit is what has grown around the ones who have
Hamtramck or nothing as a preview of a concrete flower to come.

TO PARIS: FEAR OF THE HEIGHTS REACHED

Oh I came up from anywhere
from underground, brushing the dirt
from my hair and knees, and climbed
the long stalk of the road until
it flowered in confusing petals. I
thought I was lost in its light
shadows, in confusion of ways
and absence of felt pattern. I hoped
to find a way back out again
but was so lost I found
the heart, place, square, monoliths, and fountains
bleeding with honey out of which the city grew,
bowing away in plan, petal on petal,
as a chrysanthemum of sunlight.
Oh I felt out its day's commitment
to the sun and how it shone itself
throughout one night. There was
the sky above it, high although
the flower of the city was up high.
Oh I stayed out the cycle of its day,
drunk on its juices, sneezing its dust,
and shaken by the order and complexity.
I was convinced that it was beautiful
but left it: it was not for me,
so I came off it and am back
down where I came from on the ground.

STABILITY BEFORE DEPARTURE

I have begun my freedom and it hurts.
Time opens out, so I can see its end
as the black rock of Mecca up ahead.
I have cut loose from my bases of support
and my beasts and burdens are ready, but
I pace back and forth across my right
of way, shouting, "Take off! Move out
in force!", but nothing moves. I wait
for a following storm to blast me out of here
because to go there freely is suicide!
Let the wind bear my responsibility.

WINTER: FOR AN UNTENABLE SITUATION

Outside it is cold. Inside,
although the fire has gone out
and all the furniture is burnt,
it is much warmer. Oh let
the white refrigerator car
of day go by in glacial thunder:
when it gets dark, and when
the branches of the tree outside
look wet because it is so dark,
oh we will burn the house itself
for warmth, the wet tree too,
you will burn me, I will burn you,
and when the last brick of the fireplace
has been cracked for its nut of warmth
and the last bone cracked for its coal
and the andirons themselves sucked cold,
we will move on!, remembering
the burning house, the burning tree,
the burning you, the burning me,
the ashes, the brick-dust, the bitter iron,
and the time when we were warm,
and say, "Those were the good old days.'

POEMS THREE

(1967)

● ● ● ● ● ● ●

FLOWER GROWER IN AQUARIUS

I fell away toward death
for lack of company and goods:
no business but to flinch.
A woman caught me with the hook
her smile wore at its edge
and wound me up with a winch.
Love's bucket, I was refilled!
So I came back and kissed
and cursed her. She fixed lunch.
She gave me solid grounds,
the company of laughter,
and the water works. Oh I
recant! I should invest
in fly-by-night concerns
while I have flesh to risk
and currency to burn,
so I will hang around
her wellhead and decant
death's water to my drawer.

ON BEING OUT-CLASSED BY CLASS

You   Where I came from is torn down,
say   where I'm at is condemned,
"You   and where I'm going to
can't   is not built up yet. My Grand
be   Father steamed away from yours
any   for eats! regards! and joys.
good   Better to be Dugan the Cop
because   and never talk about a shitty past
you   than to be classed out
aren't   of the potatoes in the old
some   sod. He dreamed America up, and I
one   played Indian against
from   his cowboy lies because:
some   tradition is for the rich
place."   to love, the clerks
Ha!   to ape, the poor
                 to suffer, so I wander
                 to take the air, regards, and joys.
                 Where are they? You
                 will tell me. Anyone
                 free of your slavery
                 is better off in his own,
                 so Up the five-hour day!
                 Up art! Up the I.R.A.!

AGAINST A SICKNESS: TO THE
FEMALE DOUBLE PRINCIPLE GOD

She said: "I'm god and all
of this and that world and love
garbage and slaughter all the time
and spring once a year. Once a year
I like to love. You can adjust
to the discipline or not,
and your sacrificial act
called 'Fruitfulness in Decay'
would be pleasing to me
as long as you did it with joy.
Otherwise, the prayer 'Decay,
Ripe in the Fruitfulness'
will do if you have to despair."

Prayer

You know that girl of yours
I liked? The one with strong legs,
grey eyes, weak in the chest
but always bouncing around?
The one they call "The Laugh,"
"The Walk," "That Cunt," "The Brain,"
"Talker, Talker, Talker," and
"The Iron Woman"? Well,
she's gone, gone gone, gone
gone gone to someone else,
and now they say that she,
"My Good," "My True," "My Beautiful,"
is sick to her god-damned
stomach and rejects all

medication. What do you do
to your physical praisers that
they fall apart so fast
or leave me? She needs help now,
yours or that prick's,
I don't know which.

> "I have worked out
> my best in belief
> of the rule, 'The best
> for the best results
> in love of the best,'
> or, 'To hell with it:
> I am just god:
> it's not my problem.'"

I will sit out this passion
unreconciled, thanks: there are
too many voices. My visions
are not causal but final:
there's no place to go to
but on. I'll dance at the ends
of the white strings of nerves
and love for a while, your slave.
Oh stupid condition, I drink
to your Presences in hope of sleep
asleep, and continuity awake.

What do you do if you meet a witch?
Move! from the scenery of belief in her
by air, by car, by foot, by back-
roads if you must, but move! Leave!
And if you can't or think you can't,
Oh build a fort of reason in her country,
and walk the battlements of stone,
of brick, of mud, of sticks, of thorn-
bush if you lack, and say the charm:
"2 plus 2 is four," a truth so true
it laughs: "Tautology! Tautology!" before
the numbers change in speech and come
in screams, in shouts, in lalling, or
in curses if you hurt. 2 plus 2
is Noah's Ark, with every couple in it
coupled into one and crying differently
to make a third, a fourth, a fifth, a litter.
Dove, find us a land of peace and ease.
Come back with a bomb or burning bough
proof in your claws that love or death,
in giving us the business, gives us all.

POEM

A man applying gold leaf
to the window's word backwards
combed his hair to charge
his gilder's tip with static,
so he charged his hair with gold.
He was electrically the gold-
haired father of the gold word
GOODS! and god of the store's
attractions. When he waved his maul-
stick I went in to buy
the body of his mystery.

NOT TO CHOOSE

I should be someplace else!,
but pace around in the sweats
of inhumane endeavor and its trash:
goods, deeds, credits, debts.
Have it your own way, life:
I'm just here to die, but I
would rather live it out as a fool
and have a short life in contempt
and idle graces, but, instead,
the office telephone goes off
and voices out of its dark night
command me, "Choose, Choose,"
while women's angel voices call
the cities and their numbers. Then,
when I do choose: "I run away!"
the shop door opens and a cop
or statue stands there in the way.
What does he want? Blood. Oh
let me tumble in the wards, bolts,
and chambers of a police lock locked
so I can get to sleep again,
warm in the guaranteed steel!
Instead, I have to fake him off
with promises to pay. Cash!
How cold action is. I should
do spiritual exercises toward
the body of this world
and get in shape for choices,
choices, No! Instead, I leave
the dirty business by the back

window, climb down the fire escape,
and sneak off out of town alive
with petty cash and bad nerves in
an old Ford with a broken muffler!
So here I am again, July,
vacationing in your country broke,
in debt, not bankrupt yet!
and free to get your message!
What is it?
To begin again in another state!

Ah to be alone and uninhibited!
To make mistakes in private, then
to show a good thing! But that's
not possible: it's in the Close of life
that towering Virtù happens. Why
be absent from the wheeling world?
It is an education! Act by act,
Futures materialize! So, go deal,
old bones, enjoy it while you may!:
eat, drink, think, and love; oh even work!,
as if all horrors are mistakes,
and make the social product: new
invisible skies arriving! full
of life, death, insanity, and grace!

The red curtain moving in the still room
is frightening in portent to me housed.
The heart, in its choice cage of ribs, pounds
as if the air, which was a hurricane
all up the dangerous Atlantic coast
with gross waves and accumulative clouds,
has petered out into an indoor draught
telling the officed brain, high up inside
the dead air of its hairy capitol dome
but sensitive as a bat to every draught,
that revolutionary storms are happening down there!
to move the red curtain in the still room.

MEMORY OF OLD FORMS UNDER HELL'S ANGELS

The old road followed
the lay of the land
to fords. It went
commercially to towns
around it, curving
in respect to rocks
and skirting pastures,
but the Imperial Road
denied the map relief
and spanned its rapids.
It crossed and climbed,
regardless of contour,
straight as a weapon
should be. Now,
with both disused,
and armed pilgrims
walking cross-country
to avoid the air's
condors and fliers, who
can say which road
travelled the better
to what end, or how
the travelling was
that got us nowhere,
under hell's angels.

A HOPE AGAINST POLLUTION

There is smoke over the river at the end of the street.
Something is happening, because the air is full of news.
An arriver or departer is arriving or departing and
displaces tons of water up against the rotten piers.
The gutters run with it. I hope that she or it
will bring or take a cargo of the manifest goods
and not that plague that goes from there to here
or here to there in rats' nests in the bilge beneath
the blue and white flag of the Scandinavian sky.

QUALIFICATIONS OF SURVIVORS

Hide in cesspools, sleep well
on broken glass, and eat
shit. Kiss the whips,
hold the wife for rape,
and have good luck:
stumble behind a lamb
before the bomb bursts
and crawl out of the wreck
to be the epitaph:
 "The good ones die first,
but I am not so bad:
Americans are worse."

ADULTERY

What do a few crimes
matter in a good life?
Adultery is not so bad.
You think yourself too old
for loving, gone in the guts
and charms, but a woman says,
"I love you," a drunken lie,
and down you go on the grass
outside the party. You rejoin
the wife, delighted and renewed!
She's grateful but goes out
with a bruiser. Blood
passions arise and die
in lawyers' smiles, a few
children suffer for life,
and that's all. But: One
memo from that McNamara and his band
can kill a city of lives
and the life of cities, too,
while L.B. "Killer" Johnson And His Napalm Boys
sit singing by their fire:
The Goldberg Variations.
So, what do a few crimes
matter in a neutral life?
They pray the insignificance
of most private behavior.

ON ZERO

The man who first saw nothing
drew a line around it
shaped like a kiss or gasp
or any of the lips' expressions during shock,
and what had been interior
welled from its human source
and pooled, a mirror perilous.
That was the mouth of the horn of agony,
the womb all matter tumbled out of in the first
meaningless avalanche of the concrete,
and I'm afraid that it will be
sewer of all water and the grave of space
so as to be complete.

When his head, dead tired of its theory,
dropped to the mark it made,
his forehead drank the kiss of nothing.
That was not sleep!
His students dove through it
down oceans of absence and
are not remembered, but
beautiful wet women ran out of the surf, subtly changed
and laughing over something secret they had learned.
Their navigating sons
sailed past horizons of the sensed
and founded wonderlands!
deep in the deserts of flesh away
from heaven's waters. They have not returned either.

I am not interested in mathematics
as a way of knowing, but
once I was the bravest acrobat
ever to leap through burning hoops!
Now I balk when I run at
my burning mirror, mouth, and twin,
afraid that I will not break out again
the other side of death,
applauded, unscorched, and agrin.
Oh I refuse that lovers' leap
through spit and image
down the throat of shock
and into the opposite day.
I am afraid that parity is lost
and nothing wins.

Once I calmed
myself before that chaos caught
so weakly in the charms of will
and called it cornucopia, cloaca, or else: nought;
but now the charmed
circle seems no longer to be charmed;
its wizards must have lost
the mumbo-jumbo that could call up
useful salamanders, fiends, and witches from the pit
and hold them helpless in the will
and tractable to Liberal errands.
Now when the fouls appear
howling and snorting fire,
who is to ride them out

fairly and full of honor like the knights
and to what businesses?
Whole governments of them
induce it at the world's heart,
all their citizens are food,
and it can drink the oceans,
eat the mountains, roots to peaks,
and bubble to the outer edge of air
to be a nova. "Istimirant Stella!"
strangers might say, and make their own
unearthly, efficient prophecies.

After sleepers first touch zero at the maw
they wake up in a permanently different light.
They wear its caste-mark as another eye
incapable of sleep or hurt, and burrowing inside.
They're fed to it; it
widens unastonished and they drown: internally.
If only I knew a woman's charm I cannot learn
in whose clear form and lines
the trouble of the problem slept, solved,
oh they would have a lid against its light,
rest in the mystery, and a chance
blindly to venture on in time,
but no such Cyclops
crazed by the price of size
would search the bellies of his sheep
to thank his blinders and their flame-sharp stick;
his eye is the condition of his flock
and his flock is his food and fleece;

so: sack the world's
unfinished business in your balls,
Ulysses, and escape
to soaking Venus or the red plains
of Mars: Nothing might be here.

POEM

What's the balm
for a dying life,
dope, drink, or Christ,
is there one?

I puke and choke
with it and find
no peace of mind
in flesh, and no hope.

It flows away
in mucous juice.
Nothing I can do
can make it stay,

so I give out
and water the garden: it
is all shit
for the flowers anyhow.

SELF-EXHORTATION ON MILITARY THEMES

"Courage!" I say. Thus exhorting myself,
I say encouraging words the way the lame
Tyrtaeus was supposed to have been paid
to say them, making marching songs to make
whole Spartans march away in whole faith:

> "Now hear this, you sons
> of Hercules: God is on
> our side, so make believe
> black death is white as day.
> Dress up your hair for war
> as if for girls or boys
> and throw your bodies away:
> Love and your death are equal joys."

But in his own crippled song to himself,
"On Marching Lamely," he paid himself to say:

> "Go it alone, kid.
> Run your own races.
> But when they say, 'Shit!'
> squat and make faces."

All these men later died. His and their fame
goes on in all military routines,
while the counter-song I make him say
of army verse I've said and heard
goes on in enlisted men's latrines.

Statement	*Accounting*
I too was born out of a lion's mouth	1 slice
and have the twenty-one longitudinal marks	2 slices
of passage through the teeth to prove it:	8 slices
Oh I am split up the middle half way,	for the fingers
and once up either side, further up.	8 slices
These four strips got split up into fives each	for the toes
at their tips, since once the head was out	
and chewed to features, then the teeth	
began to close, firmly: they clenched	
around the fingers and the toes. I pulled out!	
But where the main cut of the center teeth	
began, oh it is ragged and still hurts	2 slices
or wants or hopes, I don't know which,	for the penis
and strives to grow together in a whole.	(the
It's stiff in tantrum with this wish	balls
from time to time, since I was what was all	fell
there was inside the lionskin when I shucked it,	dual
and would come to you, love, past divides,	in
So when you see some hero's face	desire
framed in a lion's jaws and teeth,	later
do not be so impressed by valor's clothing,	on.)
Beast's puke, let him endure the tortures of undress.	—
Vomit your essence, Hercules. Be me:	21

FOR AN OBLIGATE PARASITE

Mother!, I am sick
of alcohol and grown up
foods. That blue milk
diet that I used to suck
is what I need. If you
give up your sour weeds
I will tear out
my permanently biting teeth
so we can be attached
again as sucker-shark
and shark, I mouthless on
you, and you savagely mouthed.
Oh we will course the Deeps
as pure efficiencies
where life obeys its first
imperative of desire: eat!,
and not the second: screw!
Oh I will close my eyes
so tight they disappear
in trusting sleep: who needs
them? Wills. Lovers. You.

TWO HATREDS OF ACTION

1. Hero

If I were in the belly of the whale
I'd praise the peristalsis of my death
and play the bleeding cilia, I felt,
like clappers of my hopes' carillon! But
once I have been downed I find
the swimming hard in acid, hard among
the downed ferocities of sharks,
my swallowed brothers, so I war
with the living dead. Terror of peace
swallows the praise, because my parts
will go to feed the beast. Sharks and I,
once we have chewed identity to shreds,
will be Leviathan, the that which eats
the carnivores in combat through its bowels.
Sleep in its body and blood! That's all
the stomach joy there is among toothed souls.

2. Coward

I won a precious I
from selfless sleep. The bells,
whistles, and alarms of dawn
awoke me. Oh I was scared
and hung around in hell:
an Idyll. Then the flags
and brass band of the day
began to fly. The opted I
was drafted and fell in

behind the chest-boom of the drum
or public heart. I drummed within
and marched away, while my true love,
who gave the word to start,
ran weeping by my side.
Fifes drilled through my ears
and found my trouble: brains
coiled in the greys of self,
and reamed them with the shrieks
of civic cadence. Forward! I
was forced to march,
up to the point of fire! Halt!:
Did I win out of sleep
just to be worked and slain?
No! Oh I would rather sleep
well out of uniform,
be slapped and shouted at
by officers of the day,
and win my death at ease,
not in the army game!
but I say what the drum says:
boom. The fifes squeal WE.
My brains are drummed out
of the corpse and wheedled away.

ELEGY FOR A PURITAN CONSCIENCE

I closed my ears with stinging bugs
and sewed my eyelids shut
but heard a sucking at the dugs
and saw my parents rut.

I locked my jaw with rusty nails
and cured my tongue in lime
but ate and drank in garbage pails
and said these words of crime.

I crushed my scrotum with two stones
and drew my penis in
but felt your wound expect its own
and fell in love with sin.

EXPENSES

I choked my frog on human crumbs.
My mother fainted when she saw
a toadstool growing from my thumb
and would not let me out of doors.
I drowned lead soldiers in the sink.
My parents fought a war downstairs.
My father lost me with a wink,
and grey pushed out his chocolate hair.
I found the toilet much too late
and stole away on roller skates,
hoping to find a cheaper law
behind the penny candy store.
I have the honor, love, to be
your animal, but will not please.

THE BUTCHER!, BORGES, WHAT A SHOCK!

For Donald Mark Fall

> *We have been well*
> *and truly had.*—Pascal

What a jewel the view
is from the furnished room,
flashing with red, green,
and orange traffc lights:
That's dancing!, and it sings
as a general sound. What
a crystal air is,
metrical in structure,
clear in the open-work,
burning at its joints,
and moving in its bodies ordered everywhere
as force's products in pure chance.
What an honor to be in it,
even as a flaw, Oh
fracture of a tree in solid quartz!

Oh I had to look away
and down the open trap-
door in the center of the room,
into the cellar hole
where I have not yet fallen.
The man-faced bat-winged worm
looked up from his work
on my love's corpse falling,
his grin foul with his lights,
and said, "So what?, Faller,

I come in the works
of your love's wounds, foaming.
My sperm are his worms.

Love, I have known
you in your change
from spring to garbage, so
I ask you. Why
is the world so beautiful?

It has to be all sex
to make us want it here
against the worm's brief:
"I am the root and teeth.
What you dream I am.
You are the meat.
Fly if you can."

So: Beget sons against death.
Get real estates against decay,
and praise physical glory!:

The stars above the roof
are there as God's dust
at the center of this sphere
whose edge is nowhere.

—*from "Pascal's Sphere"*
by Jorge Luis Borges.

POEM

The Pythagorean Silences
opted for the flesh
and came and burned in it.
They thought, felt, and watched,
wanting some ecstasy.
Oh unaccountable spirits,
they take this on as choice,
get fated, and become,
out of their nothingness,
cropping summer of delight.
They like to burn in the sun.
There is, oh nervousness,
no granary at night:
the flying chaff of the stars
should demonstrate this thesis.
They like this life and death
and stare out of the stone
forehead of a horse
as if it were some sport.

ON GAINING A SOUL

As I explained the rules,
quarters, and conveniences,
the bloodless animal
I'll call "my soul"
tongued at my blackest tooth
in absent-minded joy
and asked about the truth
of feeling: it has a short
vacation in the flesh
and everything to do,
so I should take great pains
to satisfy the guest
so that it does not leave
before I make it pay.

ON A SNAKE

The snake on the blue
pool table of the moss
is denser than a stick
of equal girth and heavier,
for all its lightness and
slick ways, because its
muscles organized beneath
the overlapping platelets of
oiled parchment have to be
compact to make that tense
wobble of reaction that
you feel if you should pick
it up. Now that I know
the motto: DON'T TOUCH SNAKES,
and wear the diacritical marks
the two fangs make, I say,
  "Man, you are smarter than it,
that muscular intelligence:
snap off its head!" The glass
snake, weighty and complex
in otherness, must think
the whole thought of the cold
when it is cold. He would
not know the drag end
of his tail from twigs
around him in the snow
when you are wiser warm,
dreaming of venom by the fire
where a cautery instrument
turns red, and healing rum
roars when the poker is dipped in.

BAREFOOT FOR A SCORPION

The color of the sac and stinger of the scorpion
was red, and got its beauty from their poison. Bare
feet ache with the threat, the eyes with praise,
the serum for revulsion. Praise be, then, that
the armored teardrop searching on the tail
could miss feet, sting sight, and reconcile
death's stamping panic with a vision of form,
red at the point where chance and law join.

IDYLL OF ASCENSION

Clicking in rock pasturage,
the deer were delicate except
for grass sounds in their teeth
from nervous grazing.

Rightly addicted to shock,
fangless economies like these
mooing advocates of speed
posit a lion in ambush;

lying down with him
in ravin's daily dream,
they struggle out of flesh
under his padded paw.

"I am undone," sings the lion,
and leaps. His Worship
drinks at the throat's race,
swills in the hollow gut

spilling with sweets, sick
with private desire, and takes
the pasture-price for flesh:
his noble joy in rending.

So it all goes, upward
like the deer's pop eyes;
whoever devours the lion
tastes the deer's flavor.

ON A HYMN, MISPRINTED

Oh they were doing custom
slaughtering down Dead End Road.
Because I am a soldier of the Gross
I went to see
the soldier of the Lamb
get his. Such eyes!
such chops! such skin!
Oh shall I fear to own the cause
or blush to speak its name?
No! It's Murder! Murder!
I sail through bloody seas.

After the engagement they stacked their arms,
wrapped their hunger in the old stains
of lousy bandages, and fought themselves asleep
beneath a white-flowering tree.
Its bark was black with clear rain.
The red heart of peace, pecked at by a dove,
hung hidden by the flowers on a high branch
the way a ham is hung up from the dogs
to cure. Why hang a heart up
in the white disguises of a black-barked tree?
The birds will get it. Also: flowers fail: once
shaken harmonically by shots or shouts,
they fall together, or they shrivel in the stench
rising from the soldiers' dirty sleep
and fall to bare the red peace of heart.
Irregulars, arisen frightened in white rain,
go jump for it, grinning like dogs
because of want. They shoot it down
as an edible beast, or as a target, or
as something else to shoot. They make
their wounds gape and utter fearful cries.
They make the bird fly off for other forage.

POEM

The tree was wet with the moon's
red water when two souls
came down from flight outside the air.

They cried at the fall to flesh
among the snapping dogs on land
and the crawfish in the water

by the tree. Their cries condensed and held
as one dove on and one heart hung
from two different branches. The white dove sang

its love of hearts; the heart
wept blood at its danger. The night
turned blue to be the moon's lungs,
and the red tree its bronchia.

POEM

Oh that was not a scrap of flying Daily News
falling on the wind
that some kid caught
and held up laughing from a snapping dog:
That was the dove itself come down
to be the pigeon for the day
when captured love grows up
to any life it has in goods and children.

VARIATION ON THEMES BY ROETHKE AND ELIOT

The child signed the steamed pane
with his nose and fingerprints. He drew
a heart's shape, the initials
of a beautiful stranger, and his own,
pierced by an arrow that was clear and cold.
The power of his waiting changed
to light: the lights came on
inside and out, it was so strong,
and then the smell of women, food,
and householed pee was changed. Cloth
came in with short whiskers soaked
in beer, tobacco-smoke and air-
smells from the business of outside.
Strength moved through the rooms
laughing too loud and hard
for the long bead curtains of rules
around explosive plates and cracking chairs.
First as a marsupial of pockets, then
as a freehold bird swung in the air,
his knowledge of the world of god
expanded in a space too small for joy.

ON ALEXANDER AND ARISTOTLE, ON A
BLACK-ON-RED GREEK PLATE

The linear, encircled youth
acclaimed his limits running
in the bottom of a plate
with "he's a handsome lad"
scratched anyhow around
him as a joke or hint
of love. A northern prince,
finishing his cereal beneath
a Grecian tutor's smile,
would see the one clear line
appear, become a youth,
and run off on the way
from breakfast to the city
through an alphabet
circumferenced by art.
This is doubt's breakfast
in a school of Gordian knots:
in ending at the genitals,
where it began, the line
is doubled on itself and tied
unclearly in a bow knot
with dangles. The lewd
scratches mar design well.
Which way can princes turn
with The Philosopher behind
them and the Greeks in front?
If cooks can shatter art
then love is menial, and boys
can use it to be gods
in thirty-some-odd years.

That was doubt's breakfast
in the school of Gordian tricks:
 "To have good government
thinkers should form the king,"
so when he took his way
he took Real armies with him:
Athens crumbled in the Seen
of Alexander's sober frown
and tricked his looking to go on
to Porus and the elephants
and drunkenness in Babylon.

NIGHT SONG FOR A BOY

Lock up the church,
I feel as unasleep
as a dead cat: regards
are what I want,
regards, regards, regards.
A priest after boy's ass
feels better than I
do: When I walk around
ladies on the stoops
think I am death: If I
had steel plates on my heels
Oh they would know it.
I should rape a saint
and she could save me
from the dangers of life.

FOR LISA

May flowers of dirt and
flowers of rocketry both
be in your bunch, love,
when you get married out
beyond my death to you
and the world's wars.
Agreed! Oh she agrees
to anything for laughs,
love, and being danced
to records playing dances.

ADVERTISING IN PARIS

On the old bridge, the bridge
they call "New Bridge,"
a model wearing the brassiere
named "Triumph!" posed
on the archaic stone.
Novelty and persistence meet
in formal beauty
and what wins? The river.

ON WORK

The smell in the diamond morning was
of a restaurant cleaning up. Two men
carried a container full of slops
to a commercial garbage truck
and drove the night-time tares away
once appetite had made the day.

Portage of day from night to night,
I had hoped to sit in the staring sun
at bitter ease, cool in the tares
of will, and also wonder how to be
not part of it, the cartage, slops,
and increments of day. Who is to eat

with such an attitude?, wooing the world
with claims. Porters and their freights
form in the aches, so I must carry three
pieces of paper and a ball-point pen
from one desk to another for profit
while there is profit under the sun.

POEM

Always prudent but unprepared
for spontaneity in weather,
the office workers got their pressed
survival jackets soaked
while running in new rain
from work to travel home.
Some of the typists laughed
to feel real water not
from taps: they are the ones
with joys to dream of, once
the day is typed away. Once
I'd hoped to dream in the rain
for life, unbothered by
the economics of appearance,
and I did, for years, and knew
its soaking intimacy. Now
I'm pressed in the synthetics too,
and have no place to go
to in the weather, except home,
but it is not so bad,
pacing an empty office after 5
in the trash of squalid crises.
I hit the key of "I"
on a girl's machine, and see
that it is red, nail polish red,
with her device of getting on
beautifully for survival:
that is not just vanity!
I get rebellious for the truth
of outside weather often, but
my check is here each Friday.

NOON'S WORLD

The day is full of people, Sun,
walking around the staring noon
of paid endeavor: it is a shock
to someone who has slept apart
all morning in a shaded room
to come out into traffic. I
am hopelessly in arrears. I try
to catch up on the action, eat
a lunch for breakfast and pretend:
What have I missed except life?

POEM

A man with a box walked up to a woman with a boy, gave the box
to the boy, said, "Don't drop it for a change," and kissed
the woman, sucking up her rosebud from her mud-color. It bloomed.
He said, "Let's go." They went, with technicolor haloes of the usual
around them. Why? Because: They come from a star, live by its light,
and burn with it here in the dark outside of the department store.

THE ATTEMPTED RESCUE

 I came out on the wrong
side of time and saw
the rescue party leave.
"How long must we wait?"
I said. "Forever. You
are too far gone to save,
too dangerous to carry off
the precipice, and frozen stiff
besides. So long. You
can have our brandy. That's life."

"Be alive," they say, when I
am so alive I ache with it
so much I do not look alive
but chase that cock-teaser till
my balls so ache with her
that I fall groaning into speech
and write the one word RAPE
on subway lavatory walls
while she, receptive but to me,
dances and sings around me:
"Yes and no and maybe so
and everywhere all over." Oh
my nonsense: she's the truth;
I cry the sentence of the Fool:
  "I don't know what to do!"
Her left eye winks Yes,
her right eye stares No,
and her smile smiles smiles
while I write copy for
her disappearance on the air!
as "Miss Unknowable, 1964."

CONSPIRACY OF TWO AGAINST THE WORLD

If I were out of love
and sequence I would turn
the end of love—its death—
knifelike against myself
to cut off my distinction and
rejoin the Commons, maimed.
But love is here!, so by
that contact with the one
oh may I contact all
self-alienated aliens
in Atom City and apply
to join the one big union.
Workers of this world, unite!

NOSTALGIA FOR A LANGUAGE

Once, when I liked a German girl,
hating the Krauts but loving the tongue
in a loving mouth, I'd make her say
"Apple!" that crucial word, and feel
like Tenzing and Hillary on Everest,
  breathless and drinking hot lemonade
    to a victory dried out of nationalism,
      class, and caste, and drunken back
        to the Garden's original purity on the heights!
Later I lapsed into hate and lost
the taste of her mouth in division.

THERE HE WAS

on horseback, and
the saber's drawn,
lunar acuity
cut out a slice
of sunlight in mid-air.
He whirled it once
around his head, a halo, and
discharged it at a foe.
Charge forever, hero! Rear,
horse! The saber points
toward death, by means
of which he changed
into a statue in the square.
To you the glory, brother,
and to us the girls.

NARCISSUS II

I used to beg for roses in the garden of love
and got them. The couples laughed and paid.
Not any more. Now the ladies do not smile.
Their gentlemen draw swords and order me away.
I went to look in Narcissus' public pool,
weeping and asking why. I had a beard! I saw,
and heard the answer: "Figure it out for yourself:
you must have grown up blind to be a fool.
Isn't there something you should want to do
or die?" "Oh remarkable absence of joy, what is it?"
A sword broke surface toward me, point first.
Then her hand around the hilt appeared,
and then herself, smiling. "Here it is," she said,
"from point to hilt and hand: take it either way."

POEM

It is no wonder that new lovers run
rice gantlets to Niagara Falls
or to some other elephant wonder:
once weightless love finds bodying
in the archaic landscapes of the flesh
it needs proportion in its flow
and goes to public waters. There
it falls asleep unoverwhelmed
while fall sounds shake the panes
of Sweetheart Cottages & Darling Hotel,
and wakes up ordinarily disposed to say:
"I gained ten pounds!", "We never got
to see the Falls!", or, "All is well."

    Oh put the elephant in chains.
    His must is dangerous.
    Three tons of love in pain
    run trumpeting over us.

POEM

Flowering balls!,
roses are coming on
in solar systems oh
galactic rose bush. By
tomorrow, given rain,
roses will be out for bees.
It's yours and mine, wild
rose, to open to for love,
its stingers and its rain,
but it is Its always.

HIS HANDS HAVE FIVE KNIVES EACH

The birth of Seventh Avenue
from Varick Street at night
is out of surf, all moonshine
as it breaks along the curb,
coming, flooding, and falling away.
In it, matter's savagery
extrudes a civic fault, a man
wading in moonlight blocks
away, hunchbacked in the shape
of things before my birth,
beyond my death, and now,
panicked by night alive.
I fear the animal embrace
of Venus' negative half-
creature of the universe,
whose wildness, let in out of love,
must be the genius of this place.

SAILING TO JERUSALEM

On coming up on deck Palm Sunday morning, oh
we saw the seas the dancy little tourist ship
climbed up and down all night in cabin dreams.
They came along in ridges an horizon wide!
and ran away astern to the Americas we left,
to break on headlands and be called "the surf."
After services below, the pilgrims to the east
carried their processed palm fronds up on deck
and some of them went overboard from children's hands.
So, Christ: there were the palm leaves on the water
as the first fruits of the ocean's promised land.
They promise pilgrims resurrection out at sea,
though sea-sick fasters in their bunks below
cry out for harbor, order, and stability.
This is the place for it! The sky is high
with it, the water deep, the air its union: spray!
We all walk the water just below the decks
too, helplessly dancing to the world's variety
like your Jerusalem, Byzantium, and Rome.

NORTHERN STATEMENT FOR ST. CECILIA

Now that autumn is over and all
that increase has been reaped or wasted,
a dead tree and the dead vines on it
scrape together in the wind as strings and bows.
This is so it can be said of listeners:
"They heard playing," before the snow
falls thicker and thicker until the air
is all snow. Then, when we dig out
of it into the upper air, those sounds
will have been buried from the air
and we will hear the silence above the tree.
This is so it can be said of listeners:
"They heard silence," not: "They never heard
a thing about the music underneath them."

A TRIAL

Two main diseases, con-
sciousness and dreams, demand
it, a division of the whole.
Then the flesh weeps to itself alone

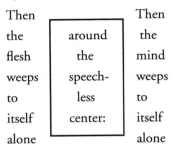

around the speech- less center:

Then the mind weeps to itself alone

That by this simple split
the subtler be rejoined: then
flesh sings in its throat,
the speechless center spreads
its wings, and Nothing says
an eagle! taking sustenance
from animals of the ground.

JEWELS OF INDOOR GLASS

The broken glass on the stairs
shines in the electric light.
Whoever dropped the beer
was anti-social or too drunk
to sweep it up himself.
So the beauty goes, ground
under heel but shining, it
and the deposit lost. But
by the janitor's broom
it is still sharp enough
for dogs' feet, babies' hands,
and eyes pierced by its lights,
that he should curse the fool
and I should try to praise
the pieces of harmony.

"I HAVE MET THE ENEMY AND I AM THEIRS"

I have found my figures,
love, and I am theirs
to do with as we will.
Oh they got sucked into the void
spaces of an infant skull
because a storm blew up in there
around a cataclysm: birth.
They fought as winged lions
until they fouled the waste
with carrion and living jaws
and almost died: their ghosts
still roar around on the air
above the desert floor
but leave objective room,
lamb, for your material:
love. Oh it is here
that I propose to build
it, the cathedral "Abattoir":
it is a concrete fold, in plan,
with columned lions to mark
it, set in a desert storm.
Please be its visitor.

POEMS FOUR

(1974)

● ● ● ● ● ● ●

I. BUSINESS JACOB, THE ANGEL WRESTLER

Not to avoid him but
to try him rightly armed
is why I go around

sweating with business while
an "I" sits sound asleep
wisely in full awares.

It waits for a touch at night
touching its terrors, to
reply: "Here is your man,

Angel: wrestle him fed,
housed by the working day,
and clothed in currency,"

but only hears a voice
laughing and going away,
saying, "No thanks,

I don't fight punks."

II. COMMENT ON "BUSINESS JACOB, THE ANGEL WRESTLER"

You can't win, you can't draw,
sometimes you can't even lose,
but even to train up to such a fight
is Victory. That man is lucky who
has even had his challenge listened to:
he can go out at night sometimes
and play around with the beasts,
and not get locked indoors to sleep
with the women, children, and slaves,
dreaming: "Isn't there something else
that I should do or die? What
have I got to lose except securities?"

MORNING AT SPEED PRODUCTS

The operators stood around the cold shop
and coughed at dirty morning jokes about
the mysteries of family life behind
them and the certainty of work ahead.
Then, when the bell rang, they each resolved,
"No man should work, but be,"
and went to cut their wrists inside
the safety handcuffs of machines.
Each man was doing life in dreams
for wages, some shit's profits, and his own
payment on his dreamed family plan.

PRAYER

God, I need a job because I need money.
Here the world is, enjoyable with whiskey,
women, ultimate weapons, and class!
But if I have no money, then my wife
gets mad at me, I can't drink well,
the armed oppress me, and no boss
pays me money. But when I work,
Oh I get paid!, the police are courteous,
and I can have a drink and breathe air.
I feel classy. I am where the arms are.
The wife is wife in deed. The world
is interesting!, except I have to be
indoors all day and take shit, and make
weapons to kill outsiders with. I miss
the air and smell that paid work stinks
when done for someone else's profit, so I quit,
enjoy a few flush days in air, drunk, then
I need a job again. I'm caught in a steel cycle.

SAINT MONDAY

Without a raincoat
I can not go out
looking for work,
so I sit in the kitchen
looking at old snapshots:

the dead at parties
or at the beach,
you nude at three
reading the *New York Times*!
Love, it is winter again:

the summer broke us.
I might find work
before next Sunday
so we can take a stroll
with money in cold weather.

ON A DISPOSSESS PRECEPT. I

"We are being torn down.
Everything must go," the sign
in the downstairs window read.
They have the laws and pries
on their side; we have
dear rubbish from the year
one. It will be pushed away
in baby carriages at gun-
point to a relocation elsewhere,
out in the dumps by The Kills.

ON A DISPOSSESS PRECEPT. II

There are rats disguised
in baby-bonnets in
your baby carriages, mothers,
so don't suckle: save your teats
for a following generation.
Where have all your babies gone?
To join the revolution. They won't last.

DEFENDANT

Someone kicked him so he limped.
Someone hit him and his flinch
shriveled his spine. He crawled to court
in answer to an ad that read:
"Justice, to be done, demands
some practice on whoever comes
in any way bent to her hand."

UNTITLED POEM

The city is empty, like a dangerous area,
except for me. One side of the street
is light: that's moonlight: that's the moon.
If I should meet a page of newsprint
flopping in the gutter like a stranded fish,
who else is there to say which one of us
is the noisier alien of this street.

ON LEAVING TOWN

This must be a bad dream. We will wake up
tomorrow naked in the prior garden, each
entwined in his particular love. We will
get up to natural water, fruits, and what?,
a gambol with the lions? Nonsense. This
is petrified obsession, perfect in tautology,
visible in the smoke, the layout of the streets,
and prison buildings. The city has put on
glass armor in rock war against its death,
which is internal. It rides out radiate
on country roads to ride down enemy foliage.
Why? There's nothing left in it to kill
except its people, and they look thoroughly every way—
left, right, front, back, up, down, and in—
before they cross another, or its streets. Such animals,
joyful of desolate beauties, they are so tough, the live ones,
that they stand around like Easter Island statues of survival won
by casual struggle, proud of their tension or their craft.
Oh I reject the dream but not the city. I
have loved its life and left it and I am
a better animal for having learned its ways;
but it is not enough to be a captive animal,
social in town. Escaped emotions: boredom and fear.

PASSING THROUGH THE BANFORD TOLLS

Proceeding sidewise by inattention I arrive
unknowingly at an unsought destination
and pass it by wondering: what next?

ON VOYAGE

Always getting ready to go out
but never leaving, I looked out
at the developments of the day
from morning up to noon and down
to afternoon and, after that,
night. "To take off," I said,
"always to leave, to begin again,"
but I stayed in my paces and room
always getting ready to go out
but never leaving. Ah how I worked
my youth away to send word out
to the day about my situation. Then
it sent back steamship tickets and
a hammer of images forged by deaths,
the idea of death, and cash, the savior.
"I have broken through," I said
to the window for the last time,
and walked out on to the ocean and
Europe for a closer view of home.

HEART ATTACK IN BAD AIR,

so stumble, heart, under the weight
of heavy air and loss of teeth,
hair, eyes, veins, arteries, balls and all,
plus living memory. Ah let them all
go bad or gone and grin the grin
of the infarcted man. What's left
of positive identity except
the papers in the wallet in between
the heart and hand the cops find?
Oh I had wanted something else
besides due bills, a passive position
under the state and on the sidewalk
under circling red lights in yellow air
while heaving prayers to the long green.
When someone steps on my eyeglasses,
however, I find I do not have to care.

UNTITLED POEM

Let them take to the air before
it leaves, and afterwards, to space.
This rock is alternately wet or dry,
iced or dusted on the surface, hot
at heart, and withering. They,
they say, are going to the stars
in office, seated at a desk
in uniforms of solid air
and senseless, but for instruments.
I might be blind naked, but I know
the star of earth is literally internal.

The independent subway of the mind
must go beneath the crust and beds
of rivers, lovers, and the dead
to hunt, as end, means, and cause,
the star they say they're flying for,
straitjacketed in padded cells inside
a weapon, watching face-mask television.

ON THE LIQUIDATION OF ZOOLOGY

We put the mountains in the valleys,
the oceans in the deserts,
and paved the world flat.
The botanical trash was burned,
and life put in its place: zoos.
In this way we cleaned up
in honor of the flat out
continuity of the green glass sea
and walked on it like Christ
in horror of the bad old days
when any kind of life ran wild
and men did as they pleased.

RISING IN FALL,

the mushrooms feel like stiff pricks made of rot.
Oh spreading glans, what
a botanical striving to butt
hogberry branches and leaves apart
to rise to fuck the sky so fast,
six inches in, up IT, with dirt
on top of each umbrella ribbed beneath,
in one night after rain. Stars,
there is life down here in the dark.
It wants you, upward, but not much.
The mushrooms die so fast
in their external manifestations that
their maggots working to be flies
make moving liquid of their blackening heads.
Oh you can see them falling downward for a week
to dirt—that's when they really live—
and then the flies take off.
How high do they get to sting us?
Not high. It's ridiculous. I ask
a woman, "Do you get the point
of all this pointless action?"
She answers, "Naturally. Yes. Idiot."

ON LOOKING FOR MODELS

The trees in time
have something else to do
besides their treeing. What is it.
I'm a starving to death
man myself, and thirsty, thirsty
by their fountains but I cannot drink
their mud and sunlight to be whole.
I do not understand these presences
that drink for months
in the dirt, eat light,
and then fast dry in the cold;
they stand it out somehow,
and how, the Botanists will tell me.
It is the "something else" that bothers
me, so I often go back to the forests.

PORTRAIT IN THE FORM
OF AN EXTENDED CONCEIT

A coal mine is a hollow tree
upside down for miners
every spring. The leaves,
whose edge is sometimes coal,
eat dirt for natural gas,
but the roots breathe air.

"Hit bottom and find it
rock to build on," it is said.
He dug where miners
wish away their lives
for daylight, pitted in the leaf.
They surface for a night of it,
high in the airy roots
and wash the naked smuts away.

Not him. He said. I quote:
"I cut the last step down
to a permanent landing, praying
for foundation in the depths,
but after each step down,
after the last, I have the shock
of unexpected falls in sliding shale."

Architects in earth
turned outside-in
despise their galleries:
they dream of bulk,
not holes. They want
to build in rock

what others float on surfaces,
and sap their plans
with soundings. Visibly,
he looked like slag-heaps
and a bitter tipple,
a machine plus waste
whose act is out of sight.

Strict as a meander,
unforethoughtout,
his sculpture of neglect
is deadly hollow underground.
Oh it redeems his curse of self
and tool-sounds down the shaft
with private profit, luxuries,
since an efficiency
for groundless ends
can tool another use:
the roots are upwards, but
some place is earned below
by self-lit slaves of his company.

RESOLUTION OF HESITANCIES

Over-elaboration of scaffolding
is fool's construction since the work
itself is always unbegun.
I could top out on my high plans
and fly the flag with the device
 "Grief for lost chances" over all
preparation, but at my age and without
reasons or children, I go to work
to lay the first stone, no more, no less,
and hollow of all contents and effects,
to be the headstone of a triumph carved:

"Cornerstone, I $\left\{ \begin{array}{c} \text{have} \\ \text{might} \end{array} \right\}$ come through."

THE DARK TOWER

*After George Gordon, Lord
Byron, the revolutionary
democrat and lover of
Greece, 1788–1824.*

The swamp around the tower was alive
with animals and was an animal itself.
Everybody looked at everybody; things
felt out things until it was Resolved:
Who is the strongest. Then the animals
attacked, ran, or fawned; the swamp
held up its tracks or let them drop.
The old black keep which I approached
past fawning animals on solid bog
was no more awful than a broken tooth
except for the man who has it. I knocked
to test his nerve and stake my claim
to what is mine by nature, his by name.

UNTITLED POEM

I never saw any point
to life because I suffered
all the time, but now
that I am happy or bored
for whole days out of pain
I regret my past inactions.
Oh I could do nothing else.

I am almost too old
to learn about human life
but I try to, I
watch it curiously and try
to imitate its better processes.
So: First pleasures after hard times,
Hello in time for goodbye.

UNTITLED POEM

Speciously individual
like a solid piece of spit
floating in a cuspidor
I dream of free bravery
but am a social being.
I should do something
to get out of here
but float around in the culture
wondering what it will grow.

Morning: from sleep to confusion.
Celebration of relevant anodynes.
Gymnastic pacing. Elimination. EAT.
Read the paper: politics: interesting:
personal intervention ineffective from
Marxist-Leninist point of view.
Go to work. Work. COME HOME.
Moment of clarity: Meet god.
Conversation as to the relation
between being and becoming.
Some relation. Whiskey. EASY.
Read. Sleep before morning. EAT.
MAKE MONEY. MAKE SONS. DIE.

Thanks for the moment before dreams.
Moment of clarity, relations,
work, conversation, god,
whiskey, sleep, thanks, EASY.

ABOUT THE PSEUDO ST. DIONYSIUS

For him the cosmos was a pearl, hell
contagious at its center, and around it
a burnt-out crust of earth
cooled but not cured by wild salt water.
Then, set as seals against this ill,
in laminated spheres in turning spheres,
rose heavens of pure shifting light.
However, he despised such jewelry,
and through the ninefold veils of shells
that censored him from love, he prayed
to burst like trees from seeds,
slowly in final Spring, and reach the heart
of the empyrean self-curing oyster-god
who should be everywhere beyond his search,
holding his flaw in brilliant quarantine.

UNTITLED POEM IN TWO PARTS

I

When I woke up with my head in the fireplace
I saw the sky up the chimney. "No clouds",
I thought. "Good god day, what did I do
last night to wake up in these ashes fortunately cold?"

Nerves, nerves, the sky is coming in to land
but I don't care. What I can't stand is conversation,
so I rape myself in retrospect and have a day.

II

There are effects
of mine all over. What
I did I'll never know
but should retrieve
my acts by their
debris, right? There are:
clothes on the stairs,
a broken window, trash
cans in the flower-bed,
a woman singing "Hi
honey", and what else?
I must have left
by the broken window or
I broke it with her head
and then came back.

Echoes of shouts on the air
are proofs of another self:
I walk around to find
it. Oh I don't know
what happened but I wish
I did because I did it,
right? Wrong. Is
everything all right?
Yes. No. Rest in the mystery.
Begin a new day.

UNTITLED POEM

Two shots down and I'm exalted,
so I have the choice: do I give out
the passion of the day to whiskey, arts and crafts,
and lose tomorrow's to the shakes and nausea,
or do I be a joiner with the bourgeoisie
and cool it, feed, do labor, and make sleep?
Ah how I envy my iron-gut youth
when I could drink and talk all night
and get to work next morning, work the day,
and come home to a woman saying honey.

LOVE SONG: CLASS ANALYSIS

I was raised in the suburbs where spite is the child of love,
and mortgagors worked out a doubted safety with their lives.
I heard them whisper of the threats implicit in an alien smile
so it's no wonder that I ran away from such a patrimony
in pursuit of alien smiles, and found a foreign girl to love,
immigrant to my hate. I felt that she could help
me to come through to love beyond that class of property,
but I am what I am by birthright, she is no longer foreign.

She is the knife-thrower's lady:
around her outline
there is a rage of knives.
Unharmed, he hopes, inside,
she is love's engine
of dark business
and the target of design.

What does she think of this?
The same, reversed: money is money
and spangled tights.
Those whistling knives of his
are kitchened at night.

FAMILY STATEMENTS

Wife: We'll gather all the people together
      and build the castle, layer on layer.

Husband: It's a hard birth
          a short life,
          and death forever,
          so why work?

Daughter: Yes
          and no
        and maybe so
      and everywhere all over.

COP-SHOOTING: ON A NEWSPAPER PHOTOGRAPH

She just shot him, in the Daily News,
and who can blame her? He,
a sitting cop, and she, a good,
big-hearted woman with a noble flaw:
fury. Cops who have to take their guns
home should see to this: it can
be murder. If the service of the gun
had not been home as a persuader, she
would still be private in her rages, not
as public as that bully Akilles, who,
when shown the metals of good arms,
"at once was moved to use them."

UNTITLED POEM

I've promised that I will not care about things,
persons, or myself, but I do. For example:
my house looks like a set for a New England tragedy
but it isn't. Outside it looks like a dump.
What it's like inside I'm too arrogant to describe
although we're happy for whole moments at a time
during this "life is pain" phenomenon.
Nevertheless my objects, loves and self
interfere with my own being. We should,
me and my wife, burn all this down
and start again possessionless toward death
and not together, which is nonsense. Loves,
marriages, families are stultifying in
accumulations of debris of love and artifacts.
Let it all go, as it will, upwards in the fire after death.

ON BEING A HOUSEHOLDER

I live inside of a machine
or machines. Every time one
goes off another starts. Why
don't I go outside and sleep
on the ground. It is because
I'm scared of the open night
and stars looking down at me
as God's eyes, full of questions;
and when I do sleep out alone
I wake up soaking wet
with the dew-fall and am
being snuffed at by a female fox
who stinks from being skunked.
Also there are carrion insects
climbing my private parts. Therefore
I would find shelter in houses,
rented or owned. Anything that money
can build or buy is better than
the nothing of the sky at night,
the stars being the visible past.

UNTITLED POEM

Once on the beach at night I heard the waves
of all drowned sailors organized into a plot
to kill me. They shouted "Come", or "Om,"
in a collective voice of combers. I said "No,"
though tempted, "not for a while", and left.
They have been liquidated on the whet-wheel of time
or have been ground between the moon's wheel above them
and the earth's wheel beneath. They are what happens to sand
once the sand is ground away. They have become
the lubrication of the process. So how could they say "Come",
or "Om"? They're nothing. They are life's come to death
in our mother, the ocean; so I do not want to join them.

UNTITLED POEM

Who can abide whom or what? That's
the problem of my harbor where
the goddess Liberty holds up her green
pistachio ice cream cone to all
comers and children: they have
to go up underneath her skirts
to reach the windows in her diadem
to be her living jewels. They stare out
as strangers at their city and her harbor.
They think—they're all the brains she has!—
"It's been a hard climb up here but we paid
to be allowed to, so we'll look around and leave
our named hearts dated on her vaginal walls,
and leave because it's easier going down."
They don't take her, Emma Lazarus, they don't
take Liberty, although you said she says she gives.

UNTITLED POEM

I'm in the house because
the killed dog has escaped
and barks all day
on the sand hills around us.
(The hunters are out in red
turncoats: the reverse
is black or brown, and I
mean fascism, brother, not skin.)
His only worthy opponent
is the land alligator
I sometimes see coming
down the sand road. Then
I hide in the john
and give my own
basic product back
to the killing-ground.

To buy: 1. Dog
             2. Guns

To join: 1. Fish and Game Club
             2. Police and Auxiliary
             3. The Revolution

To conquer: 1. Alligator
                  2. Loose bowels
                  3. Sleep

ON WHEN MCCARTHY WAS A WOLF
AMONG A NATION OF QUEER-QUEERS

At thirty, when the faiths give out,
and all the pleasures of light and air
go grey along with love, oh I began
to play the game: "Assumption of Faiths,"
and took up spiritual hobbies. God,
sports, and country were not enough
for one American, so I became
a joiner lapsing from the faiths.
May whiskey, money, and analysis
survive me through committee days
and may the night yield sex,
in which release whole moments pass.

As for the rest, left-left politics
was out of law, so I read books and bit
my thumbnails to the quick
in false despair: I am still here.

CONFESSION OF HERESY

Once I demanded annihilation and frenzy.
I applauded the smiles of thieves and had
a passion for debris. Lost in the traffic
of argument, I appraised skilled assassins
and preached the slaughter of the pure,
but now I'm scared and only critical
of what I once proposed to wreck: I see
vandals at the monuments I hoped to save,
experts, who exceed in self my strong words,
and call themselves the business or the state.
They grow up in the rubble of our wreck,
kill with a purist's hatred of the strange,
and feed on death, until a liberal man
must blush like a rose for holding on to one,
turn grey, and learn to shout the slogans:
"Annihilation!", "Frenzy!", just to run
the gantlets of their streets in safety
from himself, them, or other enemies.

UNTITLED POEM

I used to enjoy the night-time
and foraged in it for my goods,
evils, money, laughs, girls and all.

I was the noise insiders heard at night.
They keyed themselves into the wards,
chambers, cylinders, and locks of bourgeois sleep.

But now that I stay indoors too at night,
I am afraid of off-lights in the sky,
of surface noise, and of my own eyes

looking at me in the black window-pane.
Oh I look out for dangers other than myself,
and rescue by and from the sounds and lights outside.

I DREAMED I GOT A LETTER FROM EZRA POUND

Oh I got jammed among the bodies as
they yelled away the air, enclosed. I slept
naked between two living pains. My chin-
bone plowed the floorboards as my talk,
all teeth, chewed at the salt ankle of
a raving man. I have been sent here
to commit the psychopaths to violence
and have succeeded. I have my disciples.

WAR DUTY

Through the left lashes of the left
corner of the left eye, a flicker: wings.
The right eye, blind in reserve
on the reverse slope of the nose,
reports nothing. The command
center of the brain commands: No
corroboration. Hold fire. No
retreat, no advance, no war, no peace
until it can be stated: "Dove
or avenging angel binocularly seen."

ON VISITING A VETERANS HOSPITAL

Even if a man has been
chopped down to be
a basket case and has
gone mad with it, he
doesn't lack honor nonetheless.
After such actionless accidents,
honor adheres to those
who spend their subsequent lives
mindlessly singing of before.
So why not give the man a shot,
empty his bed-pan, or let him out
of the army and on to the street
to beg for women, money, and pleasure.

STENTOR AND MOURNING

Sunday was calm and airy
but artillery over the hill
made us too nervous to like it.
Some private tacked his tin
mirror to a palm tree and shaved,
using his helmet for a bowl
that would not hold
much water Monday night. I wondered,
stretched out in the while,
in the sleepy diarrhea of fear,
why soldiers fear remarks
more than a probable mutilation,
and swore myself someday,
after the important war,
to a rule of disobedience
as the bravest way. Nevertheless,
the captain's football voice,
bully as acne and athlete's foot,
commands as public law,
prussian as gossip or
the discipline of smiles;
just like when Hera rallied the Greeks
as they cried by their ships:
she yelled from Stentor's mouth
and they fought again,
not for Helen and souvenirs
or even the gods' graces, but
for Greek good opinion. Now,
after survivors' Friday,
in the short weekend of peace,

I hear that why we fight
is for a buddy's safety or
for vengeance for his death, but
I hold that most of us
nurture a fear in secret,
by and large, about our states'
power: some of us,
unknown in arms, can be
Patroklos in his onrush or
Akilles in his sulk
against the private feat
of doing as we god-damned please,
or charge a public hill
to an approved early death
under the national aegis.

ON GOING UP TO SURGERY IN THE MORNING
AND IN FAVOR OF PAIN-KILLING DRUGS

The barber nurse has shaved off sensitive hair.
Another looks at the tip of her needle.
It sprouts a clean drop of ease. One
after the other, we all go up to surgery,
strapped to our pains but drugged. Time
becomes blood. It rises from the cuts upstairs.
So, human intervention in human forms
goes on to cure or kill the living flaws.
I envy everything outside the window except the stars.
They are too hot, too far away, and dying. They indicate
pre-operative concerns and mutilative traumas
afterwards. We all say, "We shall be changed,"
and will be, vanishing in a painful flash of star-time.
In the mean time, drugs could help the agonized.

DEATH'S CHICKEN, NAMED AMELIA

I used to be bothered by death,
a bird, who flapped for claw-
hold on my sick-room's window sill.
I prayed to the yellow beak
never to peck at the window pane,
and prayed to the ringing glass
never to shatter when it did.
It didn't, and I almost healed the breach
between my flesh and dreams
that scarlet fever burned through me
and went out sunning in the back yard,
recovered to a clucking friend,
death's chicken, named Amelia.
Oh she pecked grains to death in dirt
and kept an eye cocked at the sky
where I and the danger lay.
Because I fed her, she had flown
to unfamiliar heights for me,
and when she disappeared
in bad times, in depression soup,
her bones cracked in the milk facts
of my teeth. I ate her death for life,
and went on dreaming out of flesh, wise
with the wings of love sustaining me,
and beat her de-fleshed drum-sticks on my plate
in my heart's readiness for world war.

TWO COMMENTS ON
"DEATH'S CHICKEN, NAMED AMELIA"

I

It was a matter of life and death
for her to be exactly as she was,
while I lacked reason for the fear
that made me think a bird was death,
and called my appetite its cause.

II

That guilt was no catharsis:
I still fear my own death,
her death, and death's death.
"Death's death" means life;
once we kill off all life,
nothing can die, right?, so death's
dead, killers, brothers and sisters.

BOY AND EDUCATION

Going out naked in August fog
was swimming and the moon
was like a rolled-up worm.
If that was swimming what
was swimming in the moon-lake:
water of water, milk of earth, and moon-blood.

Oh he will winter seated
chalky as his standing marm.
How ocean's distillate
can salt a boy
and Education dust him.

A normal school would teach
        The Butterfly:
    Its Systematic Dusting
        Into Law
      and how it was
    a moonlight's worm
      a night before,
        but doesn't,
teaching the social system.

TEACHER'S LAMENT

The sidewalk says,
in chalk, that he
loves her. What a joke.

So fall is here
again and school
forces the issue: to sow

at harvest. It sits
the sexes side by side
to learn the mysteries

as if they could. Then
they can drive out
on first cold Friday nights

to learn their first delights,
pay later, and dream love.

To have a toothache and no competent dentist,
poison ivy of the groin and an affair,
a sprained ankle in walking country,
and going broke vacationing—these
are just occasions for cocktail party humor.
What is decisively lousy is to be
out of whiskey on Labor Day
when the liquor stores are closed
and the merchants fly the flag for blood,
not solidarity, the labor movement, and stars,
while having to go back to town to teach
what, to whom, how, and why, on Tuesday.

CONVERSATION WITH A
DIRTY-MINDED LITTLE GIRL

What's a virgin?
    You are.
Is that good?
    Good and bad.
    Those joys and pains
    your singers
    sing about
    are real
    but never mind:
    you've bought
    their records and
    will add
    to them in time.

ON A PARTY

The children hung around
and played Monopoly, getting mad
at just a game while we
talked out with alcohol and hash
about the rising cost of love and death.
At least adults can stone themselves at play
and screw behind a lock at last before
an audience of children's wondering dreams,
while they themselves must fight themselves
asleep alone in sour propriety, sober in fear
of the night coming down on them
with futures of the talking night-wind.

UNTITLED POEM

What I remember most
about her is her clear eyes
and lips talking all
the time: no conversation,
no screwing. When I tell
her that I'll write a love
poem to her she says Great,
excuse me for a minute,
I have to go to the john.

Did you make the poem.
No.

A red leaf
fell in her hair
and got stuck in it
earlier in the day.

My heart rocked my body asleep that night
but I woke up sweating with terror anyhow
at four o'clock in the morning, for the usual reasons.

MORAL DREAM

A little girl in white, gold-haired,
came to my dream and brought a gift:
it was the doll of Christ. I was elect!
not by my virtú but by dreams equipped
to take the gift. Oh Gift-Taker, Sir
Equipment to the goddess Pedophilia,
she came to my bed in long gold hair,
and what I did with her I do not know
because I slept in sleep. When I awoke,
asleep, I found her head balled in the bone
crux of my elbow's calipers. She had
a dead man's face to measure: young
Hitler's, curdled in the flesh, with black
straight hair and two front teeth
knocked out: he was the dead doll of Christ.
I felt an instantaneous tree of ice
invade my nervous system and connect
dreams' dreams to an historical reality.
Thus, I expected subsequent atrocities
and woke for whiskey and an armed life.

ABSENT GOOD GIRL, LIFE OF MY MIND

I'm alone in the house.
The wind is outside.
You're in my head.
We look out the window.
A crocus is opening visibly.
We forget dream-fucking you.
I go outside to smell it.
You are there in the flower.
You and the flower can never
know of my love for you two.

FOR A LOST GIRL

The skinny girl I never loved and lost, ah how
she pressed against me, how I pressed her so
she disappeared in me, ribs meshed into ribs,
prick into cunt, toes into toes to the heels.
She turned on our pelvic bones and settled in,
locked in my bones in itching sweetness. Then
she fell asleep, smiling. That's how I lost her.
She is the one I walk around with in the way
the marathon dancers used to do it: she
asleep in me, while I dance after a prize.
So when I hear a girl's voice in my mouth
or see another's eyelids on my eyes when I'm asleep,
it's her, so I come to her in losses of wet dreams
the wrong way, outward, not inward to herself.
It is by this love that I rationalize myself
to myself, in hopes of the death of first self-love.

POEMS FIVE

(1983)

"SPACE IS NOT MERELY A BACKGROUND FOR EVENTS,
BUT POSSESSES AN AUTONOMOUS STRUCTURE."
–A. EINSTEIN

As an individual penance when my nothing speaks
I dial the car radio on to overlapping bands
late at night, and do the stations of the breath
in one place, although the car moves at the speed of sleep.

American distances come out of the machine as one noise
fouling the time of air with wastes of music and speech
unhearable in unseeable space except mechanically
transformed by static to pollution of one's observational ears.

Then I can say to my nothing talking to itself,
"Listen to what is going on! This night atmosphere
is an articulate structure of lousy music and lies.
What do you say, why bother, who's driving, what's right?"

INTERNAL MIGRATION: ON BEING ON TOUR

As an American traveler I have
to remember not to get actionably mad
about the way things are around here.
Tomorrow I'll be a thousand miles away
from the way it is around here. I will
keep my temper, I will not kill the dog
next door, nor will I kill the next-door wife,
both of whom are crazy and aggressive
and think they live at the center of culture
like everyone else in this college town.
This is because I'm leaving, I'm taking off
by car, by light plane, by jet, by taxicab,
for some place else a thousand miles away,
so I caution myself: control your rage,
even if it causes a slight heart attack.
Stay out of jail tonight before you leave,
and don't get obstreperous in transit tomorrow
so as to stay out of jail on arrival tomorrow night.
Think: the new handcuffs are sharp inside
and meant to cut the wrists. You're not too old
to be raped in their filthy overcrowded jails
and you'll lose your glasses and false teeth.
How would you eat, study and be
a traveling lecturer if you got out alive and sane?
So remember to leave this place peacefully,
it's only Asshole State University at Nowheresville,
and remember to get to the next place peacefully,
it's only Nowhere State University at Assholesville
and you must travel from place to place for food and shelter.

UNTITLED POEM

Once, one of my students read a book we had.
She was doing a history assignment on
the decline and fall of the Roman Empire
and crying. When I asked her why
she said Because. All those people died.
I said that if you start to cry for the dead
you won't have much time for anything else.
Besides, after all the city people were killed
or died off, because their cultures got too high,
the barbarians kept some peasants alive
for their food value. Some barbarian raped
some peasant woman who produced
a child who ultimately produced you
and me, so there is this family continuity,
so don't cry, it's obvious, look around!
This is the reason why we Americans
are a nation of peasants and barbarians.

TO AN EX-STUDENT

Annie, your face is in fashion this year and so are your legs.
When I look at the child models in the high-fashion ads in
    The New York Times
I get a hard-on remembering our horizontal conferences
    at college.
I wonder what happened to you after you graduated and I
    got fired.
I remember saying, "Go get a modeling job, get notoriety,
    get around:
those of us who get around a lot tend almost inevitably to
    meet again,"
and you saying, "I had to wait around all day with two hundred
    other girls
for some raging fag to say, 'Look up, look down, let's see the
    legs, that's all.'

ON FINDING THE TREE OF LIFE

After Genesis 3: 22–23

If there is an outside out there
one should go out to try to find it.
This I did. There is a garden world
out there, with birds, trees, and the tree
they call The Tree of Life. The birds
avoid it, naturally. The bunches of red
berries are intact except for one bunch. It's
partly eaten. The spoor around the tree
is old, but it would indicate that some
stupid godforsaken human or beast
had staggered around and crawled away
in the first agonies of immortality.
It's too bad for it, whoever it is
and will be: our own deaths are bad enough.

TO A KID WHO BELIEVES IN ASTROLOGY

Those lights in the sky at night are not
from the stars as they are now. Also,
they are from where the stars were.
Now the stars are some place else
and the stars themselves are different.

Each point of light you see is the central point
of a continuously expanding sphere of light
that the star sent out once long ago
while going away. It interpenetrates
all the other spheres of all the other stars.

I don't think that it refers to you because
it all happened so long ago. You're too stupid
to listen to me, you beautiful astrologist, and I'm too
        stupid to know
what's happening out there where space is dark
and filled with interpenetrating spheres of light.

UNTITLED POEM

Our German teacher used to say
    Der Schnee gefallen ist
    und wird es weiss
when snow fell on the campus. She never would
translate a word she said: it was a pedagogical
principle with her. Consequently, I could understand
    The snow fallen is
    and "*wird*" is white
but never got to understand the word "*wird*."
Now, when I wake up to the first snow of the year
and feel like dancing in it or running around
like a child, I remember Fraülein Flola's drill,
and the mysterious word "*wird*" doubles the mystery.

APOLLO,

once, when he had saved the human race again,
said, "At least you could get me a piece of ass
this time." So we came up with the best we had
but she ran away and turned herself into a tree.
The god was big enough to honor her for doing that
and that is why we victors get you, Laurel,
though not often and most often only once,
but now, they tell me, oh my one-shot Laurie,
that you took some new boy home with you
and only come out once a year to do the shopping.
He must be some hero to be called the Mighty Oak.

TRANSFORMATION

She's changed, my six-foot
bucktoothed student in braces,
pleated skirts and knee-socks,
the way that some birds change
their plumage and songs in spring.
Her hair's down, her awkwardness
and braces are gone, and man,
does she dress! Slinky! He must
have been some quickening lover, that
married professor I saw her with
a couple of times downtown, or else he was
merely a tool of her changes, because she said,
"I'm gonna find myself a nice boy
now and settle down." Luck!

GLAD AT THE COLD (1955)

The live storm went through last night
and blew away fall. Many leaves
are in the gutters of this street
which doesn't even have a tree. I'm glad
at the cold because that wind
is cold enough to drive you back to town
the way the homeless lungers must go back
to the pneumonia wards in Bellevue Hospital.
I think I am your ultimate shelter too,
so, shiver in your suntan for a while
until the pipes freeze in your summer place
and then come back to town: there will
be some warmth here with me. When
certain November comes around with probable you
you should be solid, laughing with health,
and sad at the cold and the fading suntan.
Oh may we snug out winter in this dark
city apartment, almost underground. Then,
etiolated in spring, oh you can go
bloom in the countryside again, since I
can't even try to keep you from the sunlight.

ON A BAROQUE CLOCK

Miniature Greek gods support the Roman hour,
having nothing else to do, or hold
some dead white grapes to girlish smiles
as the time runs around in a gold ring.
Orpheus plays a lyre. Eurydice reclines,
as if the ticking rock was hell's upholstery,
not chalk-faced onyx cast with runes.
Ah Orpheus, dead youth, this is a result
of marriage: when art and wealth conspire,
like Greece and Rome, to demonstrate
that clocks count, you singers lose
maturity, voice, and size, and have to freeze.

ON HERODOTUS

It was said of Herodotus the Liar
that he wasn't blessed by the goddess Hera
at all, or given divine inspiration
as a gift, but was just a clever operator
doing his "researches" or "inquiries"
into what is now called "History"
as a more than normally fallible human.
I claim that he wasn't a liar at all:
he just made up what he thought
to be the facts. There's a difference.
You'd have to be an ancient Greek
to know the difference, so you can't.
In some cases he lied, in some cases
he told the truth, in other cases
he said what other people wanted to hear,
like any other writer, and in other cases
he just wrote down what other people told him,
although he wouldn't or couldn't understand
anyone who didn't speak his form of Greek.
You'd have to be an ancient Greek to understand
that there was no language except ancient Greek
which I'm not, so I must be wrong about all this.

THE DECIMATION BEFORE PHRAÄTA

A variation after the Greek

The army marched by for days and was admired by all
of us for its silence, discipline, and carrion eagles.
Rank after rank marched by in the right order and step,
each man heavily packed and armed and looking like the next.
Every night they built a town with towers and walls.
Every morning they tore it down and marched away.
We withdrew when they attacked, attacked when they withdrew
and lived high off their baggage train, killing a few,
losing a few—it was our same old free-style army game—
but they, those killers, had been broken into slaves
and feared their officers more than they feared the enemy.
This they were right to do: once when they broke some "rule"
before our Phraäta, we heard them beg for punishment,
so they fell in and counted off and each tenth man
was pulled out of line and killed with his own sword.
They called this "decimation" and did it to strengthen their "wills."
What a people! They killed more of them than we did, but
they beat us anyhow. Then they marched away!
They didn't take what they came for, our defenseless Phraäta.

That empire is incomprehensible, but we are in it.
They came back for Phraäta and now we are the light horse
auxiliary of the XIth Legion (Augustan) of the Empire
and have no home. The Legionnaires still shout
to their officers, "Please decimate us!" The officers
always do, as we watch, and they always win,
and we and our horses are with them on the flanks
because there's nowhere else to go and nothing else
for us barbarians to do or be: it's a world empire.

ON THE CIVIL WAR ON THE EAST COAST OF
THE UNITED STATES OF NORTH AMERICA 1860-64

Because of the unaccountable spirit of the troops
oh we were marched as we were never marched before
and flanked them off from home. Stupid Meade
was after them, head on to tail, but we convinced
him, finally, to flank, flank, cut off their head.
He finally understood, the idiot, and got a fort
named after him, for wisdom. He probably thought
Lee would conquer Washington from Appomattox
if he, Meade, should march his infantry behind
him, Lee. Ah well, the unaccountable spirit of the troops
triumphed, Meade got his fort, Grant got his presidency,
Sherman got his motto, what was it? War is heck?, Lee got
    a military school
for the education of young Southern gentlemen, and the Union
Army was taken over by Southern noncommissioned officers
in the wars against the Indians to the west. I know all
about this, I know who won, I served under them
for three hundred and fifty years in World War II,
just long enough not to be called a rookie but a veteran,
and realized the rank and order of my enemies:
first, the West Point officers; second, the red-neck sergeants;
third, the Nazis and perhaps the Japanese. I won
all of these wars as a private soldier, for a while,
and am happy to have done so: without me
Hitler and Hirohito would be ruling the world
instead of America and Russia, but I still will not
drive through Georgia with New York license plates.

SPEECH FOR AENEAS

Dido cried at the innocent fact
that I had to leave and not come back,
but a public official must be brave,
and dare the women and dare the waves

because he is bound to do his duty
to be the king and burn the booty,
so, "Peace," I said. "Your Majesty,
pity the hardhearted part of me:

a roll in the hay is good for you
but a man of gods has work to do,"
so we sailed on the earliest possible tide
and she went and committed suicide:

a great queen, and a swell dish,
and I'm sorry it had to end like this,
but an oecumenical society
is more important than matrimony.

Oh peacock, Argus-eyed and blind,
when Io, mounted by the bull,
sang "Love!" your ugly voice replied,
 "Yes I am lovely," and in a lull
in calving, oh your soundless lyre
sang: "The sweet face of the bull
is like the feathers of a peacock's pride:
both in their beauties are terrible."
No wonder Hermes had to kill you.

ON SHIELDS. AGAINST WORLD WAR III

For Paul Bowen

Ah what bastards they all were, and are,
those heroes of the *Nibelungenlied*,
echt krauts, liars and fancy dressers,
robbers of the peasants for mere money
and cowards, too. Even their greatest,
strongest warrior, that Siegfried,
is afraid to fight honestly: he has
to wear a cape of invisibility and
impregnable skin-armor to win honor.
What bullshit. Worse than Hitler, a pure, lying,
murderous slob. When he can't stand
behind his shield, the greatest in the world,
in some honest battle with some stupid
dwarf or giant he goes magic on them,
according to his anonymous hack poet,
and wins by trickery, deceit, lies.
That Siegfried is your hero, you cowards,
and I, too, have to acknowledge his nobility.

HOMO LUDENS: ON AN ARGUMENT
WITH AN ACTOR

There is a difference between acting and action.
After a bad take the killer and the killed
get up and go back to their chalk marks
and do it over again until the director is satisfied.
Some of us actors claim that action is acting.
This is too simplistic a claim, though true
in a way: we have to pretend to survive,
and stunt men sometimes get maimed or die,
Like gladiators in the Roman Games,
but if I shoot you or you shoot me, one
of us winds up in the hospital or morgue
and the other winds up in jail or escapes.
This is the difference between acting and action,
although the deaths of gladiators and stunt men
make a clear definition of the differences difficult.

FROM THE THEATER LOBBY

There might have been higher music but
the drummer made the loudest sound inside.
The ushers joked and mugged and had their hands
on all the door pulls, an actor shouted,
an actress screamed, then it was over,
over in a breaking ocean of applause.
The audience came out lit up like fireflies
and the old characters went back to sleep in their parts.
In this way the great tragedy
had fooled and boomed its way across
another Broadway night. As to what happened,
the critics will tell about it in the morning.

WHAT A CIRCUS

First I locked hands with myself
put one foot on the opposite hip
and hup! leapt up
on my own shoulders like two acrobats.
What was underneath one? Space.
I did a double take and dropped.

Then I bent down in between my legs
and curled myself in half.
My head rose up behind me pointing front,
faced by my ass in doubt. I flipped
out. The hell with this
contortionistic acrobatic act. I ache
for the time when I was neither half
nor twice my given height, but one
to any power as a standing man.

UNTITLED POEM

One tries to be sober and respectable
so as not to be committed as insane
by the extended family or state police
but every once in a while something happens
that blows the whole construct apart.
One finds oneself stripping the pants
off a litle girl who says Wow, or else
one falls down in the front yard of her
house party and cuts a forehead just to go
for more beer with the money taken from
her mother's purse. All these activities
supposedly have consequences, but
if one dresses correctly and has the right
social attitude, haircut and spare eye-
glasses it is possible to maintain that:
that that little girl raped me, that that
old lady gave me the money for beer,
and that I walked into an open car door.
If one does not have the suit and all, all
one has to do is hide out for a few days
and the scars, girl, and old lady will fade away
like the money. This is why there is no reason
for suicide, and this is why there is no god.

RELIGIOUS QUESTION

When my wife said, "Oh angel, angel, angel, you'll save me'
    in her sleep
I wondered who in hell this angel was and why
the Judeo-Christian-Islamic tradition is such a god-damned
chronic, infectious, unbeatable brain disease
that even my own true wife, my passionate atheist,
my politically anticlerical lover must dream
of an angelic love and savior to devil her sleep
and I must be jealous of her devilishly heavenly incubus.

PRAYER FOR ONE LEG

My foot is blue with blood although
my face is white. "Strip out the veins,"
the doctors say, and take my money. Now,
heart, pump up the blood to where
I need it most, the brain, and down
to the scrotum's bodily Golden Mean.
If I can't walk, then only brains
and come can move me out of here.
Oh my third fist and driving force, dear heart,
is it because I have been arrogant
toward any of my members that you give
the most blood to my proletariat,
the feet, to keep in gravity
and do not irrigate the whole?
I know that blood can go away and leave
the pains of stone-aches, head-aches,
due to the improper exercise of love or thought,
so I conclude that I have not
loved love enough in the balls, or thought
enough in the brains, fists four and five,
so may I have a life afoot somehow
with crippled courage, lovers, and ideas.

PORTRAIT

What a beautiful young man,
everyone says, although his lips
are blue from cyanosis. He is
brilliant and well informed,
cogent in argument, witty in talk,
startlingly honest and fair,
courageous in person, loyal to friends
and loved by many women
for his physical beauty, directness,
frank use of a good blue penis
and ethical position: Stick
to one woman for as long as it lasts.

It's too bad that, since he knows
he's dying of a known malignancy,
he wants to be an artist but can't
and won't have children but can.
All the women tell him this.
I can't tell him anything but if
I could I'd tell him: "Have the child
your women want, or "Teach while you can
or at least think out to children
about what's going on in your body:
we all have to die but you
know it positively at what? Twenty-five?"

UNTITLED POEM

Why feel guilty because the death of a lover causes lust?
It is only an animal urge to perpetuate the species,
but if I do not inhibit my imagination and dreams
I can see your skull smiling up at me from underground
and your bones loosely arranged in the missionary position.
This is not an incapacitating vision except at night,
and not a will of constancy, nor an irrevocable trust,
so I take on a woman with a mouth like an open wound.
I would do almost anything to avoid your teeth in the dirt.
She is desirable, loving, and definite, but when I feel her up
I hesitate: I still feel the size of your absence. It is
as large as the silence of your invitational smile
or the vacancy open in the cage of your ribs. Fuck that,
I say. Why be guilty for this guilt? It's only birth control.
Therefore I extend my hands tongue and prick to you
through her as substitutions for the rest of my body
in hopes that you'll be born again as her daughter
before I have to join you as your permanent husband,
but I know you: you want me to come, come as I am,
right now, without her, and to bring along a son.

SUMMER HEAVEN, ANGELS, HEAVEN

"It's as if they're glued together,"
his mother said to her mother
who said, "How revolting,"
as they watched their newlyweds
not quite fucking on the beach.
Young, pretty, thin, fair, brown,
they didn't go away on honeymoon
because they wouldn't leave their parents,
so we'd find them screwing in our beds,
on our lawns, or on the beach at night
like those permanently fucking angels
in some early Christian versions of heaven
or like Plato's vision of the beast with two backs.
Later they settled down, immaturely:
he went to work for his father,
her mother mothered her babies,
but oh what a one summer they had had,
before they went to sit, still pretty, with
the grown-ups on the beach, and watched the kids.

IN MEMORIAM. UNFINISHED.
FOR ROBERT BARLOW. 1950

This anthropologist had learned
Mayan and Nahuatl
and had a good theory
of Mexican Culture growth,
disproved by now by new diggings.
He had a white horse as a gag,
servants who fought with knives,
and taught at a tourist school
in México, D.F.
I didn't like him much
but he was a human being,
gave easy tests
and did not kill more
than he had to, so I'm sad
he died instead of his
accuser: a student said he was
a fairy and got expelled.
He had a nervous breakdown
and flew to Yucatán
where the folk seem mild
away from violence
in love. It was
his crisis of maturity
and he muffed it, saying
to his father's fathers' sperm,
 "This is the end of the line:
all out," there, where the priests,
he said, would ring
church bells at midnight
to wake their Indians to love

away from suicide in conquest.
With his round glasses
and two buck teeth
he looked like the Mayan glyph
for the day "Two Rabbit,"
but was strong in science,
field work, and teaching.
Later, some of his verse
came out in *Poetry* (Chicago), set
in the smaller type because
it was unfinished like the life,
the works, and these regards.

UNTITLED POEM

When the window glass blows in
and your books jump off the shelves
into the puddles from the shot-out plumbing,
don't pay any attention: paying attention to losses
has no survival value. Instead, return fire
but take evasive action: if a hole
occurs in a wall, leave by means of it
if it is out of the line of fire.
The clothes you're wearing will be your uniform
if you get out; if not, they're just clothes.
Remember that your pistol is your best friend
only as long as it or you have bullets.
One could almost pity the man who shoots
his last bullet not at himself, accurately,
or else call him a stupid masochist because
he'd have to go to the enemy's electricians
to have his deepest convictions broadcast
at full volume to a small audience
of critics who insist on revision, revision.

PORTRAIT OF A LADY

She is no longer the argumentative type of campus radical
always screaming at committee meetings and student strikes
and fighting to get control of the mimeograph machine.
Oh no: now she's ladylike and respectably dressed,
she carries secret messages in her Tampax, laundered money
in her hollow heels and an explosive and expensive
handbag wired to her gold wedding ring all because
they sent her her boy friend's penis in a box marked
Official Gov't Business in order to destabilize the opposition,
reduce it to mere counterproductive terrorist activities
and, later, to demonstrate the efficacy of their new
strip-search techniques to their covert funding agency.

It's like being a winner at an all-night poker game.
I know I can't leave winning without getting beaten up,
so I go on playing, trying to lose a little, but not too much,
hoping that mutual exhaustion will stop the game in the morning
when the coffee, the bennies, and everything else
that keeps poker players awake
has given out, and it is generally agreed
to stop the game because of fatigue.
Then, I can take my winnings and walk away, carefully,
after giving a cut to the loser who follows me
and wants to break my arm,
and go home to sleep like death and dream
that my patience and expertise and money and winning
makes me a hero. No way. They know I have their money.
They know I'm a winner. They can get me if they can.
I know I have to play in the next game
for safety's sake, and try to lose a little.
It's difficult, they're such a bunch of dopes, but they're my boys.

SCENE (1946-7)

The poor kids are active in the penny arcades.
They murder commies and dead ducks.
They can stop a bear in his tracks
with one ray of light and win
prizes to prove it; in their photographs
from the four-for-a-dollar photography booth
she holds a doll, he wears a lewd tie,
and then, ah well, you know, they go home
not even together, the poor children, they
should steal a car and go screw
in the back seat, not the front,
because of all the problems presented by
the steering wheel and manual gearshift.

UNTITLED POEM

I love the way the heel of my hand feels
as it moves down her spinal column
to the beginning of her ass. She is
a beautiful but also a rich woman, so
we artists and writers pay court to her.
If I really got to the ass I could marry her
and make a million dollars in alimony
after the obligatory divorce. I really like
the way I feel she feels but I could not
put up with her accountants, lawyers, children
 (especially the children) and ex-husbands, but,
the way she holds on, the way her back
seemingly yields and plays at the turn of the curve
of the small of her back where her ass
starts to form harmoniously when we kiss
at one of her fund-raising cocktail parties, oh if I
could explore that territory for a while
I would give up my primitive Marxist philosophy,
my dedication to poverty and hatred of the rich,
and almost become the liberal of her own dreams.

UNTITLED POEM

Consternation in household!
Arrival of telegram.
Somebody died. To
Occupants: Please comply.
With what. What's
going on out there.
What is important is: Is
the door locked. Have
the neighbors seen. Are
the curtains drawn. Who
goes out to see. You,
he, she, it, not me.
Mama, put on
your powder, rouge, lipstick, stockings, high-heel
        shoes, flower-print dress and white hat,
and then go out. Pretend to shop.
Buy something. There's nothing
wrong with that.
Let's see your smile.
Go find out what
is going on out there
and then come back.

VARIATION ON "WINTER'S ONSET FROM AN ALIENATED POINT OF VIEW"

The first cold front came through Indian Summer
and blew the autumn foliage show away
along with the drunks, addicts, crooks
and weaker regulars from Washington Square Park.
The "Please Help Disabled Vietnam Vet"
who had been sleeping on the warm sidewalk
by the drugstore that sells the ha-ha cough medicine
has had to leave for warmer vents. Where,
I wonder. If he drank another bottle of that stuff
oh he'd be warm enough for a while
in the southern California of its first gold rush.

ON WEARING GLASSES

No more football.
To wear glasses
is to look for truth
because glass lies,
doubling the visions
of the inaccurate eyes'
lack of contact lenses.

When they blindfolded me
my mother held the handkerchief
my father tied the knot
and I got turned around.

They laughed and snuck away
and when I tried
to find them I could not,
but I knew what
they went to do
and where they went to play.

When I got bored with blindman's buff
their handkerchief became my wife.

God help the eyeballs which
are waters in red caves.
When they get weak and pervious
they must be faced with glass
and set in frames.

God bless optometrists,
by means of whom
I first saw stars
and fell for a visible moon.

That first optical vision of night
showed me the competition: stars
in a field of excellence and the moon
perfect in outer form but vague
as to its inner features like your face
approaching, Beryl Howell, when
I took my glasses off for my
and your first kisses on your own
doorstep to an expanding universe.
Thank you. It might be
in a state of collapse. It can
be slightly penetrated for a moment.

UNTITLED POEM

The patients in the waiting room
are nearly silent like the hanging plants.
Once in a while one rustles or sighs.
A sunbeam moves across the floor,
climbs the wall, hits the NO SMOKING,
NO MEDICAID sign, and disappears.
Subjective time collapses and expands
like a new four-dimensional model of the universe.
The doctor and his machines
conduct a long painful diagnosis
in a back room. They have found a new
interesting malignancy, and take their time.

UNTITLED POEM

The doctor and I have become intimate.
He has wheeled me off to a dark room
where we can be alone together.
He hums "For I Am a Pirate King"
from *The Pirates of Penzance*
as he pries out my eyeball
and lays it on my cheek. "Don't flinch,"
he says. "You could hurt yourself that way.
I start screaming, "Black Eye Patch,
Black Eye Patch. Pirate. Pirate."
He says to stop screaming. What
will the patients out there think?
"I can't give you an anesthetic just
yet because this is just a diagnosis
but don't worry, you won't feel a thing
during the operation." "I thought this was
the operation," I shouted. "Silly," he said.
He fondled my eyeball and gave me a soul kiss.
"This is just the beginning of our relationship."

THE SUFFERING OPHTHALMOLOGIST

I thought he was torturing another patient
in the back room as usual because
of the groans and whines until
I realized that there was no one there
but him, singing to his hemorrhoids
in the john. He came back to the examining
chamber, smiling and chatting as usual,
and did his usual job on my eyes,
but I had some Schadenfreude as I
walked out blind into the daylight: that
guy has his agonies too, just like,
but not where, the ones he inflicts on me.

ON BEING ASKED HOW DO YOU FEEL AFTER
AN OPERATION WITH INADEQUATE ANESTHESIA.
THIS IS HOW I FEEL:

I.   Richard Nixon
is standing
in his underwear
in the South Bronx
in the rain.
Bob Alplanalp
and Bebe Rebozo
are pointing at him
and laughing.
He's crying
with gratitude.

II.   Richard Nixon
is standing
in the South Bronx
in the rain.
He has lost
his underwear.
He covers his parts
with his hands
and smiles shyly.
Something has gone wrong.

III. He is surrounded
by black children
with walkie-talkies
and knives.
They are waiting
for the market

to settle down.
Eyes opened low
in mixed trading.
Kidneys are sluggish.
Penises are slack.
There are no calls
for hard-ons.
Nixon has a hard-on.

IV.   There's a call
from the Burn Unit.
Fresh skin is wanted.
Premium prices
for whole skins.
Hard-ons optional.
The flayers scrub up.
Nixon autographs himself.
He is cloned
the hard way
but cloned.
He or his clones
will be the next Presidents of the U.S.
That's how I feel
since you asked:
much better.

ON CABIN FEVER,
ON BOREDOM IN THE COUNTRYSIDE

I've been outside to see the countryside
but feel, So what: it's only a vision.
Inside in the dark it's not much better.
Experience, external and internal, is
not so meaningful. How I wish
for a great cause or a great love
with which to pass the time in a great way.
I watch the cat. It watches me.
It is not bored with its boring life.

I go on, too, in persistence of life
for biological and perhaps other reasons,
but I have to fear death and expect
something else once in a while like everybody else
although I'm bored or hurting or both
most of the time except for those split seconds
of ecstasy which might be meaningful
and seem to be, no matter how infrequent
they are and how impossible to understand.

TO A COLLEAGUE. FROM THE COUNTRY

I'm jealous of your life. What
are you doing out there. You're
probably having a drink at that
bar and trying to get into you-
know-whose panties and joking with
those friends of yours I don't
even know while I am sitting here
all alone in the snow having no
fun. Man, man to man, I hardly know
you so why are you doing this to me.

ON HIBERNATION IN THE COUNTRY

This semi-permanent drunken coma is agreeable.
If death were anything like this, I'd buy it.
It is either boring, delicious, or nothing with
occasional hot flashes of terror or joy.
The rest of it is solid, productive sleep.
It could be better than being too alive in spring,
the way the birds are to any possible
hawk in the sky or snake in the grass
waiting to take their selves and families.
The birds are not religious about this
the way I would be if I were religious:
It's just the way they have to be to survive
the spring activities. So the hibernation's not
so bad: with sleep you save on the food
and heating bills, and as for entertainment
there's the interior television of old nightmares.

SUMMER GALE

This is my last
message for a while:
all dates are off.
The wind is high,
time is nearly up,
everything is blowing
monarchs to pieces,
so bye bye butterflies.
What a process
of common disintegration.
Goodbye, I might
be back from where
the wind is blowing
but not in time.

WINTER GALE

The old joints of the house
cracked in the gale but the house
held around the bass chimney.

Your pet pine tree has flown away
with your outhouse. I hope
no one is in that flying coffin
or else there'll be
shit all over the landscape
and a free funeral
attended by a pine tree.

My weakest windowpane
has given out and gone
to join the ceremony in pieces
and the prayers of my breath
go with it. What a bloody flux.

UNTITLED POEM

The Monarchs, the butterflies, are commanded:
Go take a flying fuck: Make worms.
This is their own form of intercourse.
I watched a couple for a while
but got bored: watching others' passions
is strictly for biologists and voyeurs.
When they finally did get separated
after the hard work of the ecstasy
they flew off separately immediately
looking for edible flowers in a breeze.
If one or both of them survive the swallows
who can snap the body of the bug and let
both of the wings drop perfectly intact,
oh they could fly for thousands of miles
southwards on our strong north winds.

UNTITLED POEM

One used to be able to say
what Seneca said to Nero:
"However many people you kill
you can never kill your successor."
But now the joke may not
be necessarily true: we might
have done it already. So let's
remember what the poet Oppian said:
"The hunting of Dolphins is immoral
and the man who wilfully kills them
will not only not go to the gods
as a welcome sacrifice, or touch
their altars with clean hands, but will
even pollute the people under his own roof."

AFTER A POEM BY CARLOS DRUMMOND DE ANDRADE TRANSLATED BY ELIZABETH BISHOP AS *DON'T KILL YOURSELF*

Listen, Dugan, don't read.
It's bad for you. Don't hang around
reading bad novels indoors, drinking
yourself to death on carcinogenic beer
and going broke. Do something. Stop
being an idiot, stop living
off women. Be a man, not
a gigolo. Go out, find a job:
the day is interesting outside,
there are all sorts of people,
actions, scenery, and things to do.
Life is not that difficult!,
to do and die of, so go out, pretend
to love it, leave it, or engage in it.
Go buy something, razor blades,
a woman, a politician, a god;
steal some money (basic), do
something, don't just sit here reading and writing.

LAST STATEMENT FOR A LAST ORACLE

After this oracle there will be no more oracles.
The precinct is hereby desanctified. You wanted it,
you have it. From now on everything I say
will be a lie said for cash. Now, for the last time,
here's the truth: You have won with your horse power
and numbers from the north. You will go on
winning forever—this is your damnation—
until your conquests and the insides of your heads
are alike, and you and I know what it's like
in there, so if some dirty beast remembers,
on some future dirty night, what it was like
once to have been a human being and pleasing to me
in a fair exchange of pure sacrifice for pure prophecy
he will throw himself into a fire and howl to death.
I will now drop back into the fire you are
so curious about. When you get drunk tonight
and pee on it, it, you and I will go out like the light
and an acid yellow smoke will take the place of our souls.
We will have to go on living a lie for a while, however,
in the unspeakable condition I have referred to in passing.

APOLOGY (TO THE MUSE)

I'm so unaware of what
is going on around me that
I like to watch the brief lives
of the birds: they look around
before they take a seed because
they're always there at present,
self-accounted for in their fears,
hungers and the necessaries
of their rites, whereas I
do not see approaching cars
forget dinner and my address
and realize your beauty
only after you have made a pass
and gone away, saying, "Oh well."

UNTITLED POEM

I'm waiting for you, but not purely.
I'm not all waiting the way a dog
outside a supermarket is all waiting
for his mistress, doing nothing else
but waiting, having nothing else to do.
Oh I have something else I have to do,
I think, and I can make up things to do,
so that I am not all waiting like a dog,
but I am waiting for you, though nor purely.
So come on, come out, wherever you are
or else my impure waiting might change
to pure waiting, or into mad waiting.
I might stop waiting entirely just
when you, as you say, say "I'm coming."

NOTE: THE SEA GRINDS THINGS UP

It's going on now
as these words appear
to you or are heard by you.
A wave slaps down, flat.
Water runs up the beach,
then wheels and slides
back down, leaving a ridge
of sea-foam, weed, and shells.
One thinks: I must
break out of this
horrible cycle, but
the ocean doesn't: it
continues through the thought.
A wave breaks, some
of its water runs up
the beach and down
again, leaving a ridge
of scum and skeletal debris.
One thinks: I must
break out of this
cycle of life and death,
but the ocean doesn't: it
goes past the thought.
A wave breaks on the sand,
water planes up the beach
and wheels back down,
hissing and leaving a ridge
of anything it can leave.
One thinks: I must
run out the life

part of this cycle,
then the death part
of this cycle, and then
go on as the sea
goes on in this cycle
after the last word,
but this is not the last
word unless you think
of this cycle as some
perpetual inventory
of the sea. Remember:
this is just one sea
on one beach on one
planet in one
solar system in one
galaxy. After that
the scale increases, so
this is not the last word,
and nothing else is talking back.
It's a lonely situation.

POEMS SIX

(1989)

TAKEOFF ON ARMAGEDDON
—FOR RONALD REAGAN

As we tour the field in the pause
before the final battle, you can see
the flowers growing upside down
among the opposing troops. The roses
look like hairy turds in the dirt
and the insects are behaving like animals
gone wild in the stench because God rots.
They have stung everybody involved:
the forces of good and the forces of evil
are stuck: it's them against them,
they're exactly equal, exactly the same,
there's nothing to fight about, it's all over,
they have all been fundamentally stung.
They stand there forever, paralyzed in shit.
They wanted Armageddon, they got it.
This concludes the tour of the battlefield.

As we move beyond good and evil let us hope
a sexy hunger for catastrophe does not revive them
from their statuesque military postures because
the final battle will be, you know, the final battle,
and then there will be no more good, no more evil,
no more beyond good and no more beyond evil,
no more roses growing upside down in the dirt,
no more insects, and no more you and your rotten God.

When the front-end loader ran over my wife's Montauk daisies
I wanted to tell the driver, Butch—a nice kid—but couldn't:
"No flowers, no us. Flowers are basic to human life.
That's why we think they're beautiful. No flowers, no seeds;
no seeds, no greenery; no greenery, no oxygen: we
couldn't even breathe without them. Also: no greens,
no grasses; no grasses, no herbivorous animals;
no animals, no beefsteaks. There wouldn't be anything
to eat except fish, and no way to breathe unless
we went back to the ocean and redeveloped gills.
There the seaweeds would make oxygen by flowering underwater,
the way it used to be in the old days, and you
would be running over them in your submarine. This is why
flowers are thought beautiful, and this is why it's important
not to destroy too many of them carelessly, and why you could
have been more careful with my wife's god-damned daisies."

ON NAMING A BABY MIMOSA

Oh sensitive mimosa, you have
more feelings than most other plants
because you shrink up at my touch
but no more brains, so why
should I say anything to you? Because:
you remind me of that touchy blond
baby I love and hate, who does not
listen to me either. Therefore I say:
Go bloom your pretty flowers while,
wherever, and as much as you can,
because I'm tired of talking here alone:
I feel like the devil and god mixed up as a man,
and if you do not listen to me,
and you can not listen to me (no ears),
and if you do not look out for me,
and you can not look out for me (no eyes),
I am going to bomb your whole
dirty world out from under you
and blow your radioactivated seed
out to the stars above your dumb heads,
but you, you will not understand,
because you have (again) no brains,
or know that sunburned baby's name:
Abounding in Likeness; otiose; mime.

SURVIVING THE HURRICANE

When the neighbor's outhouse went by
and landed upside down on my property,
unoccupied, I laughed and yelled, "It's mine,"
but what's so funny? the TV says
that many, many will get blown away
in the hurricane's uproarious humors,
and now the horizontal rain comes through
my wall, the wallpaper heaves and cries
and runs down to the floor as pulp
as the windows go out with the wind,
poof!, and the wind picks off the roof
two shingles at a time in love-me-nots,
and there is no difference inside or out:
Leaning against the wall or the wind
is the same. This wet is that wet.
There is no protection anywhere except
I go stand in the upside-down outhouse
with the crapper over my stinking head,
once it has dripped dry of its storm-borne shit,
and be the dry mummy of its sarcophagus
under the whole hurricane of the universe.
That's what's so funny: Egypt.

AN ENVY OF NATURAL FORMAL LIBERTIES

You birds stay out all night
in all the weathers all the time.
Oh how I envy you
and the departure of your
beauties from the coming cold.
First five, then seven more,
that makes twelve, a flock,
uncountable in process of migration,
maybe a hundred birds go up and down the air,
working a globe, a rough one,
changing all the time in time
in various transparencies
to hit the ground without
a bounce, there's nothing:—
I couldn't see them in the grass
unless I knew that they were there.

Then they're up again. They're
black birds screaming all as one
except for a few gone strays,
and line up on the wires between the poles
in flight from spheres to flats to lines,
in flight from three to two dimensions,
from four to three to two in time:
they are so still at rest
it is all one.

Two weeks to Labor Day, you
flying fools!, the stronger first,

the weaker later in a V: That's
the natural formation flying
life to death for you! Then
you're off to Florida for the winter
in that permanent vacation of the free
you're always working at for all your lives.
Oh may I too work my passage free
and make the Key West to my desiring
when my great Labor Day arrives.

CODA

You birds don't work for strangers
because you have no hands:
you just happen to be free.
What about those other birds
who have to work their beaks,
clap wings, and dance their feet,
cooped up in cages so some boss
will throw them grit to eat?
If nobody clipped their wings,
why don't they beak the lock,
claw down the door, take off,
and head for the horizon where
your flying answers freely are.

He walked around dictating
what could be his profit
in his necessity, jingling
the balls of his coins
in his pants pockets. He
was money and money talks.
He talked and was the one
whose talk we sickened at.
Nausea was his atmosphere.
Open an office door
at his shop and Aargh!,
panic appeared: we froze.
That was his sex: he
told me when I quit:
"Power is what I want
the way you want to be
a whore. You think
you'll stop getting screwed
just because you're leaving here.
No way. You're made for it?'
He laughed until he coughed
the come of his life up
and spat it in my ear.
I gave birth to this
economically maladjusted poem.

LOVE AND MONEY

The United States of America is like a convention
        of the International Baton Twirlers Association
in Johnstown, Pennsylvania, during a steelworkers' strike
        when I went there once as a bill collector.
The locked-out mill-workers on the street corners
        stared at the nearly bare-assed middle-class girls
dressed in nothing but expensive glittery rags
        with a dirty gray lust for money and cunt,
but they didn't touch the girls or the mills
        because they weren't theirs. Right and wrong.
The girls weren't theirs but the mills were theirs
        because they built them, ran them, and made
everything in them except the money: it went away
        to where the girls were, so they stood around
without the money and watched the girls.
        Therefore I took the money and flew
back to New York to tell the liberal conservatives
        that the republican democrats are right:
There is no left-wing politics in America left.
        There is the International Baton Twirlers Association.

MARXIST ANALYSIS OF THE FIFTH LABOR
OF HERCULES

The Augean stables were so full of horseshit
that the Augean nobles came to laugh at Hercules
when he was told to muck them out by hand.
They hoped to see him filthy on his knees,
all asshole and elbows going fast for years.
Instead he wrenched a river from its bed upstream
and set wild water roaring through the place
and washed it all away, all
the horseshit, and I mean all
the horseshit, —the horseshit, the horses,
the stables, and the nobles too,
standing around ready to bugger Him,
Hercules, Wrestler of Rivers. Conclusion:
Revolting conditions elicit revolutionary solutions.

"Pray for me and die rotten," the men's-
room wall read. "I don't want a drink,"
the old whore said. "You know what I
want. Come on. Come on. Come on."
"You couldn't come if you was asked,"
the bartender said, so she walked out
screaming into the traffic but the truck
stopped: she couldn't even get run over.
"God protects them," several people said.
How the air smells best on leaving a bar
broke in the morning with nothing to do
but be at present at Liberty's harbor
under the protection of that goddess,
and sit in Battery Park and feed
my beer-nuts to her pigeons. Impossible.
The Juggernaut would never stop for me,
the way it would for the holy drunks,
so I went a few blocks north to join
the godforsaken whores in slavery.

REMEMBERING AN ACCOUNT EXECUTIVE

He had a back office in his older brother's
    advertising agency and understood the human asshole.
He turned his father's small inheritance over and over
    on hemorrhoid ads between three-hour lunches
at the Plaza every day and cocktails at five-thirty
    with different dressy women waiting in our front office.
We joked that he fucked them up the ass to make more customers
    and were nauseated by him because he picked his ears
with the lead end of his lead pencil as he argued and argued
    hemorrhoid copy with us on nauseating Mad. Ave. mornings.
Why argue? It must have been for executive power-feelings
    because the copy never changed. Every week, the poor
bleeding assholes bought the shit. When my mind
    began to get fucked and go as black as his inner ears
I quit as broke as I began, remembering his prophecy:
    that the last working television set in the world
would be showing a hemorrhoid ad for ANUSALL
    at Armageddon, that it would have been written
by him, that he would be watching it at 6:00 P.M.
    in the bomb-cellar lounge of the Park Plaza Hotel
with a blonde's ass in one hand and a scotch in the other,
    and that he would die happy, with his old man's
money intact and his asshole too, unlike us prat-boys.

MONOLOGUE FOR A SIXTH AVENUE SCREAMER

You don't know anything about city life.
Sometimes you were lucky to get out alive
from some of the places I used to go to,
and if you were lucky enough to get out alive
you were lucky you weren't killed outside the door
and if you weren't killed outside the door
you were lucky you weren't killed on the street
and if you weren't killed on the street
you were lucky you weren't killed in your apartment
because you know who you'd find in your apartment,
you you you, screaming in your toilet bowl:
        You God-damned shit.
        You God-damned turd.
    I hate the standard of your life.
    I hate the standard of your soul.

SEXIST LAMENT: RUIN BY MONITOR

When you came in the office saying "Hi
Honey, so this is where you work,"
my boss, my boss's bosses and the boss himself
stared out at me like Easter Island statues
from the television in the bugged room,
and when the bullhorn's word came down:
"Dugan, you should have kept your love outside,"
I knew I'd blown it and was in for hell.
Oh I got processed out into the gutter, ruined
with you. Good business is for gangsters organized
in fear, love, and doesn't let some girl
come kissingly to the money-works on payday.
They think that you're for lunch;
that you get bought and sold at night,
or that you're there to decorate the lobby.

EMPIRICAL SCENE

We saw a grand piano fall off a roof
as if in slow motion, and hit
the sidewalk without a sound
as we laughed at the philosophical implications
and went down into the subway
where the noise of all crashing pianos
is kept on permanent performance
at full volume, so at least we weren't deaf
or in an inconsistent universe.
It had been like the beginning of a silent movie
but we didn't know that we were in it
so we never found out what happened,
we, who didn't hear the grand piano.

ON PLUMBING AFTER AN AIR RAID

The houses have dropped their bricks
behind a screen of bomb dust
and become red rubble, fast,
where trees of plumbing stand
and bear their porcelain fruits—
sinks, bathtubs, toilet bowls—
four floors high in the air.
Oh let our hydraulic culture rise
new from our lead-pipe garbage heap
and geyser out of the fire storm
to fall back on our sewerage,
so that all lovers underground
may join their waters to the waters of life,
and the nude in the fourth-floor bathtub,
dead but sexy, and wholly exposed,
be the goddess of the city's fountain.

ON FINGERNAILS IN BLOODY TIMES

God help the fingernails:
they are cursed by atrophy
and are no longer claws,
just clarified visors glued
to tender quicks. What
nonsense that the fingers wear
shell born from the sea
and not more serious weapons.
Oh you can bite them, paint them,
scratch with them, or else
wonder why they are, by God,
but that's about it, right?
Wrong. Why do our torturers
rip them off so much?
Because they are the backups
for our grasp of things,
not just our caresses,
and are the delicate armor
over such a sensitivity
that we wouldn't even have the hands
comfortably to fight with
if we didn't have them on.
That's why they rip them off,
the pretty little fingernails.

ON A POCKETKNIFE. ON CARRYING

If only a maniac possessed it, he
could hone it on his thumb: it
could practice on a diet of split hairs
so as to flash across the flesh I fear
and make a night of ambulances and the police,
but now the rust of my neglect comes over it
like the disease of unrequited lovers in the old
romances. What catastrophes it makes me dream
of as it sharpens pencils near my skin:
Oh I can let it wander in the flesh of fruit,
but no slit throats, no hearts searched for
through the ribs, no outrage at the penis,
though sometimes I am so ashamed to waste
that passion keening from my pants' back pocket
for a course of blood, that I dream blood,
and walk at night knife-handed and afraid
to find the forehead of an innocent to sign.

Then if I anti-skate my thumb along its edge
my thumb weeps, and if it's pointed to my back
my back weeps, and if it's pointed at my front
it fills my stomach with the sweet ache
of an ugly prophecy I want to shit away
just when my cock and balls attempt to shrink
back to the safety that the running guts deny.
My face dares it. It wants the scar.
I see it flashing. I could lose my eyes.

The blade is junk except for what
it carries on its edge: the edge,

and what it carries on its point:
the point: that's where it narrows down
and vanishes: its point
and death for those it hits
is balanced on that fine frontier
between the gross shining metal
and nothing at all. That's where it's at.

TRAVEL ADVISORY FOR A NIGHT SHIFT

It is the kind of raw and changeable afternoon
when the undersides of the clouds are dark
but white on top because of the crazy weather
and the wind rolls beer cans in the gutters.
They're worth money but nobody picks them up.

The violence of the street people seems to give way
to that of the weather: they keep it all indoors,
apparently, and only the roaming New Jersey marks
in heated cars seem out for normal trouble and
the few poor street whores frozen naked to the ass.

Let those who can be warm inside be warm inside
while we, dear, get to go out dressed for a wild night.
We have to get from here to there by morning, which
is where the profit lies, and spend the night between
in making it between some pretty cold betweens.
So, let's watch it with that crazy weather in the street.

DEDICATION FOR A BUILDING

The excavation for the new
clinic of Bellevue Hospital
was littered with knocked bricks,
corrupt plaster, and old ward-
flowers thrown to the blasting-dust.
A cat grinned with the effort
as it chewed a piece of meat
fastened to a kraft paper bag
while some man slept off something.
May the new clinic rise to cure
all ills its site is host to,
and not mistreat the desperate.

OXYMORONIC HOSPITAL BLUES

I knew it was going to end badly
when you put the bouquet in my urinal.
When my nurses' aide saw it, she
yelled: "No good! Urinal for pee!
Need clean clean for test, Mr. Dopey!"
She said "Not again." I said "Never again,"
and she went to the sickroom john to clean it
while talking dirtily to three absent presences
named "Madre de Diós," "Diós Mío," and just "Madre."
She was a beautiful, small woman
to have such an ugly, large vocabulary,
so please do not contaminate
my piss-bottle with your flowers again:
it is just a classy gag
that overworks the underpaid.

BOAST

I've walked every walkable bridge
into and out of Manhattan and climbed
the towers of Brooklyn Bridge twice
and gotten the grease of the Roeblings' cables
all over my hands, face, and raincoat,
drunk illegally up there where the cables
groan on their supporting high rollers
      Hurray
and now I'm crippled in Manhattan, played out.

Should I have done a Brody
when I had the high body
rather than lie here in a flat?
No. Rather I celebrate the rain-
storm over the East River that night
that kept the police indoors
and lit the bridge with burning water
back to Brooklyn where I was born.

SOLILOQUY: GHOST DANCE FOR A CRIPPLE

Something has happened to the air: a fly
fiddled some of its hind legs together on
the white tablecloth, turned around three times,
and then turned over on its back and died.
This happened before World War Three
when everything is happening all over
and everything can be blown away.
Regardless of what Mao Tse-Tung says,
"The wild bear cannot frighten a brave man.
Even the plum tree is pleased with snow
and doesn't care about freezing or dying
        houseflies,"
I am afraid of the wild American animals
and am going to rip the white tablecloth off
the table and dress in it and catch
the dead fly as it flies through the dead air
and dance around this dead room
on my cane and good hip and bad hip,
wearing the tablecloth and with the dead fly
in my arms, in my mouth. I
am going to make fun of the whole process
because it's awful, and this is my ghost dance,
and it's all for you, but I am not
doing it: I'm a cripple: you're doing it.

PROVINCETOWN *TOTENTANZ*

It's obscene, the way you have a girl's voice
and flirtatious manner in a broken-down old body.
When we stand together on canes at cocktail parties
you say, Let's kiss, nobody kisses anymore,
come on, kiss me, I'll give you AIDS.
Remembering how you felt when you were fifty,
I could get a hard-on if I could get a hard-on
so I send you off to get another zombie.
Then we can dance together later, drunk.
six-legged, bones to bones, we'll knock 'em dead,
you, the ancient flapper, me, who looks like death,
as figures in the comic strip The Plague Years
for these kids who never knew what it was like to kiss
everybody at the party!, regardless of the sex.

IN MEMORIAM: AURELIUS BATTAGLIA,
AND AGAINST HIS TRAGIC SENSE OF LIFE

Aurelius Battaglia, the greatest loudmouth in the world,
has bored everybody to death and shouted down
everybody everywhere at cocktail parties and bars
in New York, Hollywood, London, Paris, Rome.
Now, when I meet him at Ciro's bar, he can't talk,
he's had an operation for cancer of the larynx,
he can only whisper, constantly, spitting in my ear:
he claims it's his fate, his destiny, his comeuppance,
he's being punished for the sin of hubris, of overweening pride,
he's paying out to all the people he has pissed off
by his immoral shouting domination of all conversation,
he feels proud of his own personal, ironic, and tragic fate
as the greatest loudmouth ever made silent by overuse
of his vocal cords resulting in absolutely just throat cancer.
I try to say, "Aurie, Aurie," although he cannot hear me
through his crazy whispering speculative egotistical logorrhea,
"Listen, Aurie, it's true that you have an appropriate fate,
that you're an offensive loudmouth shut up by throat cancer,
but don't really believe in appropriate fates or tragedies
or just punishments for hubris: that's just bullshit:
it might help you in your merely personal agony
but remember contingency, remember automobile
        accidents,
remember the random deaths of innocent people in wars,
politics, fires, epidemics, plane crashes, you name it,
we live like herds of animals, impersonal personal accidents
happen regardless of personal characteristics, vices or
        virtues.
So listen, Aurie, when you and I walk out of Ciro's drunk
        tonight

after the bars close, when we are still arguing this problem,
when you are not listening to me and I am not listening
    to you,
we could both get hit by one of the drunk drivers
    around here
and that would not be tragic, it wouldn't even be fate:
it would just be ridiculous: death. So, *Pace*, Aurie, *Pace*."

ON THE DEATH OF NORMAN DUKES

When the poet was dying of cancer
he had to get rid of his airplane.
He couldn't fly anymore
and couldn't keep up with the payments:
it would be a burden on Nellie,
so he had to get rid of his airplane,
he wrote it over and over
in the last month of his journal:
he knew he was dying of cancer,
he couldn't fly anymore,
he couldn't keep up with the payments,
so he had to get rid of his airplane,
he wrote it over and over:
after a note against suicide
it was his last journal entry.

ON A BENIGN BUREAUCRATIZATION OF DEATH

After my father died fighting at
my mother for life as usual,
like the yard dog with the house cat,
I thought that she would sit and hide
for months like a damaged animal,
staring and mute until she saw
his shadow moving on the wall
from some car's headlights outside,
and start to screech at his ghost
for years in the empty house
like so many old Irish ladies do
until she got put away, too,

but she went to her sister's place
next to the funeral home upstate
that her sister's husband bought,
and aged out gossipy and sweet
about the quiet, prettified stiffs
she helped to dress next door,
because she knew the mortuary talk
was all business at the dinner table,
all rational, all accountable,
and she could get a good night's sleep.

LAMENT FOR CELLISTS AND JACQUELINE DUPRÉ

When the beautiful cellist Jacqueline DuPré
died of multiple sclerosis at forty-two
all the cellists grieved, and one
fell on her instrument, not
as a sacrifice, but as an accident,
if there are such accidents. She was
hysterical, but there was no
damage to the tone, and it only cost
a thousand bucks to fix. Remember,
a cello is a beautiful shape of air
set in the right box and played by strings
played by strings the player plays:
the player can't get close to it the way
a violinist does, feeling the air play
the wood play the bones of his/her head
as the violinist joins the music to the brain.
That's why some cellists dance
with it like Yo Yo Ma, because it is
an outside music that they have to join
as athletes of a different air,
so when Jacqueline DuPré died young,
her muscles dying on her first,
it got to the cellists in their very art
because they're distant from their instrument:
it can't go to their heads, like violins.
With her, the music started distantly, then
it got more distant, then the distance
got to be the infinity of cello death
the way a cellist I knew would drape his tux
around his instrument before he went to sleep

after a performance in a strange town
so the cello could be the cellist through the night,
dead silent, with a black bow tie around its neck,
and he could joke away the horrors.

STORY FOR ACTORS

There's a story that a traveling Greek actor
came to a Spanish town in Hellenistic times
to give a reading from Old Greek Tragedy,
but that when he went on in the amphitheater,
dressed in the horrible mask, the long robe,
and the high-soled star-actor's cothurni,
and roared out the terrible old lines
the poor hicks panicked, and some of them
got trampled to death in the stampede.
The municipal authorities were so stupid
that they banned Old Greek Tragedy forever
and executed the actor for mass murder.
That they killed him for being too great
is the greatest praise an actor could ever want,
but that they couldn't even write up his name
is proof of their own illiterate shittiness
and of his immortal anonymous fame.

ON A TRAVEL STORY FROM WORMWOOD VALLEY

When French monks stole the bones
of St. Benedict and his sister
St. Scholastica out of Italy
and smuggled them into France,
they split them up because
when holy thieves fall out
there's the devil to pay,
so one set went to Le Mans
and one to St. Benoît-sur-Loire,
but they say they got the sets mixed up,
so that there are two incomplete
brothers and sisters together
in holy partial skeletal incest forever or
until they join our general incest of dust or fire
in the flying coffin of this world.

ON A DESOLATION OF THE ANIMALS AT NIGHT

I used to think that the animals
were exempt from human suffering
because they had no brains, but now
I'm not so sure because I hear
two cats moaning on the windowsill,
sleeping in a desolation not to be denied.
Why is it that the dirt made flesh
must suffer for its intuitions for a while
before it goes back to its nature? Ha,
dancy cats? Ha, sleepers? Why
are the insides of your bone heads cleverer
than opals, onyx, and Egyptian goddesses?,
in bearing witness to what's what:
those roaring horrors of the universe,
the stars, if we could only hear them
burning outside the window while you cats
sleep moaning on the windowsill as I
watch out from something wondering inside.

NOTE

This is what your cat does
while you're at work this morning:
It sits in the middle of the room
and looks at something on the ceiling.
Then it gets up, stretches and smells
the chair legs and my legs
as I drink the coffee you
so kindly left me, silently.
Then it sits in the middle of the room again
and stares up at the ceiling again.
Then it gets up again and walks
around your apartment again
smelling legs in the silence: It's
driving me crazy. When I've left,
after locking the self-locking door
exactly as you told me to, dear,
I don't think the cat will notice
my absence the way I hope you will,
you cat-person, you cat-torturer, you
member of the Spay-Neuter Humane Society,
but will be staring up at something on
or through the ceiling all day long
and smelling out the paralyzed legs
of the locked-in chairs until tonight
when you come home and bring it food,
your moving legs, and your electric presence.

WHY THERE IS NO CLASS SOLIDARITY IN AMERICA
I READ IT IN *THE TIMES.* AUG. 2, 1987

An Italian in Hackensack got mad
at the Jewish lady downstairs
and hired a Polish man with three rattlesnakes
to slip them under her door and kill her,
but her cats raised such an uproar
that the cops came and caught the snakes,
the Pole, and then the Italian
because the Pole ratted on the Italian
but who ratted on the Pole? The rattlesnakes?
One of the rattlesnakes bit one of the cats
but the cat recovered. All this proves
that there is no class solidarity in America,
and that cats are better than rattlesnakes
if they come from Hackensack and are Jewish cats.

SUBURBAN EXORCISM

When the witches' coven across the street
hung a dead rat from a pine-tree branch
across our access road, it was not for us,
it was an imitation of the crucifixion of Christ
done as a Black Mass for psychotherapy.
The witch-mother had a radio talk show
in Boston and explained it: God's rat
embodied the collective unconscious guilt
of her therapeutic community which got
exorcised as a dirty thing for mental health.
When my wife went to Town Hall to complain,
all the women in the office went Yuck,
and promised immediate action but the town
road gang wouldn't touch that stinking rat.
They took our whole god-damned pine tree out
with a front-end loader and burnt it,
so watch it: America is full of believers,
Black-Massers, witch-mothers and rat-hangers.

AMERICAN TOURIST TO A GUATEMALAN
TARANTULA

You are the black prince of bananas,
so if I vandalize your yellow
upside-down Indian palace you have
the right to violence, but if
you trespass as the hairy crack
of chaos on my hotel bedroom wall,
here I am the lord, charged
with the place and lady, so
expect some breaking furniture, shouts,
and murder dancing in my shoes.
We exploit bananas. I stamp on you.

ON A SKUNKED FOX

I found out where the smell was coming from
when I looked under the beach-plum bush
and saw the skunked eyes of a fox looking at me.
He didn't even try to run off, as if to say,

"You are one of those killer human beings I
am supposed to run away from. Here I am.
Put me out of my misery," but I didn't do it,

so he walked away slowly and sat on a hilltop
as a target, scratching his eyes with the sides of his paws,
but nobody shot him, so he walked off again,
as if looking for a road to get run over on.

CARLA IS A HORSE LOVER

Carla bought an old horse
to save it from the glue factory.
She fed it, combed it,
and rode it carefully,
but it threw her. Then it
sat on her and broke her pelvis.
Now she can't take care of it
because she lost her job
because she's in the hospital,
and people say Carla!
Sell that horse to the glue factory!
but Carla says No!
My girlfriend Simpson
will take care of it,
and Simpson does.

THE DYING SEAGULL AND THE GREAT WHORE
OF THE WORLD

The seagull sitting on the town beach must
have had a broken wing or foot: It didn't move,
with all the swimmers looking at it, when
a little girl dressed just like a child whore
in a red spangled bikini bottom and unnecessary bra
squatted down to pat it on the head.
It must have been waiting, in whole composure, for
the night's predators or the tide to take it out
to the death begun by natural breakage and
the minimal tourist attrition of the child's hand.

ON FISHING BEING A CHANCY LIFE

In Memoriam: John "Picky" Thomas

Once my wife and I were invited out trap-fishing because
the fishermen believed that tourists and women brought good luck.
When we climbed into the boat, a half-decked one, at dawn,
there was a gull trapped in the bilge, screaming. "Don't touch
that fucker," the captain, John Thomas, said. "She could
bite your fucking finger off." He grabbed the bird
by its shoulders and threw it up in the air.
The bird hung there into the wind, still screaming,
then started circling around the boat with the other gulls
so as to take part in the morning's fishing.
I was astonished by Thomas's pounding activity:
he must have weighed two hundred and thirty pounds
and had hands bigger than my feet, but
he moved with absolute delicacy and speed
in the rocking boat to throw the bird in the air
under the mottoes: "Don't hurt yourself." "Take care."
and, "A man can't be too careful of himself around here."

TOURISTIC NOTE FROM THE GULF

As the fishermen pulled up the giant manta ray
she gave live birth, and a dozen of her young
flopped back into the Gulf of México off Yucatán
where Mayan queens would pierce their tongues
with the ray's stingers, and the kings their pricks,
to keep the universe fertile and in proper operation, but
tonight the giant triangular wing-flaps
would go to every Chinese restaurant in town
for some of the identical reasons in soup:
as nourishment, laxative, and aphrodisiac.
That's what happens: the bloody old transcendence
winds up in cheap soup in a broken-down town,
and what can save the baby manta rays
from the destruction of the Gulf of México, ha?

CRITICISM OF BERGSON AND DARWIN

The primeval fish was like a squid, all mouth,
with eyes, ears, feelers, nostrils (or gills),
and ten tentacles set closely all around it.
The tentacles kept pushing food into the mouth.
The mouth was always snapping open and closed
with teeth: choppers in front, fangs at the sides,
grinders in back. Inside the mouth
a tongue was always lashing ground-up fish
and chopped-up seaweed into a rear gut.
Behind the gut there were two thrashing tails,
and between them there were two holes and a barb.
Fish bones and mash came out of one hole. The squid
put the barb into the other hole of another squid
while the other squid put its barb into
the other hole of the first squid. After a while
squid eggs came out of both of these holes,
and some of them floated ashore and became us.
What a tragedy. You lost your barb
and kept your hole. I lost my hole
and kept my barb. You get to make the babies.
Why? Why? Bergson and Darwin do not say.
Is this Creative Evolution? No. Is this
Origin of Species and Descent of Man? Yes.

SPEECH TO THE STUDENT CLOWNS
AT THE CIRCUS CLOWN SCHOOL
AT SARASOTA, FLORIDA

You innocents who want to play the clown
should be wounded combat veterans first.
You have to get the gut feeling, how,
when the fallen gladiator with a face
white in shock with two red spots
of panic on his cheekbones and his eyes
animal with black grief got the sign
thumbs down from the Emperor,
a bloody clown stripped off his face,
put it on, and danced around the ring
with a slapstick sword to tickle the crowd
as the corpse was dragged off by the heels.
This went on for centuries, centuries,
until you took up the mask and made it sad
or, worse, giggled, and made it sweet.
What happened? When serious art dies
in its wisdom, in American innocence,
even the bloody old farce of death dies.
Art must be ugly or lovely or both
to be beautiful, but not nice, terrible
in its pitiful humors, but not cute.
Ask the nasty children about this
some night before they're put to sleep
to clown around with the fiends.

ON HALLOWEEN

—after Kallimachos

The gorilla mask got put away
because we got too old
to see the face outside the face
inside, but it becomes
a Dionysius of Tragedy again
when a nephew puts it on
with the scary beast costume
and growls, "my hair is holy,"
"telling me my own dream."

INTRODUCTION TO THE TELEPHONE

The telephone rang in the grocery store
and the grocery man said Answer it.
I was six years old and did. I said
Hello to the black mouth on the wall
and the black ear screamed in my ear.
I dropped it scared as he laughed
and I lost my telephone virginity
to the black howling universe of wire
looping out the plate-glass window, down
the Brooklyn avenue to New York City:
there, a vampire self of words sucks
money from that wire world, but I
am sick because it bit me in the ear.
I am adult to the instrument
and listen to the women angels' voices
calling the cities by their given names.

ELEGY FOR A MAGICIAN

Once I got so skinny
that I turned pale blue
in places and became ethereal
against the hard knocks
of the broken furniture
in the depression years,
but when my mother screamed
at me through one ear
to come and eat my beans,
the other ear stayed fixed
to the dying radio while
Chandu the Magician hissed
and whispered me away
inside his crackling box,
up the aerial and out
into the open airways as
the blue genie of Brooklyn.

MEMORIES OF 1936-7

When I walked my nazi girlfriend
home from public school I tight-
rope walked the curbstones while she
kept to the center of the sidewalk.
Although we didn't say a word she knew I loved her
blond braids and dirndl dress.
They kept a photograph of Hitler
on the mantelpiece between two candles,
and when he called the Volk in
they went: my first love sailed to the fire,
but not before her brother beat me up
unfairly: he kicked me in the balls.
I decided to kill Hitler, and did,
with the help of millions of others
like the Jewish kids on the block
who played "Burning Hitler's House"
with cardboard boxes in the gutter.
We were premature anti-Fascists
and my Dresden doll went to our fire early.

ON THE LONG ISLAND RAILROAD SYSTEM

I used to hate to ride the Long Island Railroad trains
to Rockaway Beach on Sunday mornings with my father
when I was an adolescent. He'd make me fake it that
my I myself was under twelve and half a fare when I was
     six feet tall
and fourteen. I didn't understand, in my grown rage
at being kept a child in knickers, not long pants,
that he was broke and showing me his own youth's way
out of his dry land life in Brooklyn and dead Queens
to the possibilities of the sometimes wild Atlantic Ocean,
pointing as a one-time sailor to the East, that there
was something going on out over there beyond the surf
and crowds of human bodies, girls!, playing in it,
that might be serious, dangerous, and worth it.

AUTOBIOGRAPHICAL LIBATION
TO ERATO MUSE OF LYRIC POETRY

The baby-sized but skinny bronze statuette in a bronze
    Grecian robe
looks at a bronze butterfly on her raised bronze stink-finger
while the bronze lyre at her bare bronze toes lies unplucked
above the circular lead base where the anonymous hack sculptor
has caused to be inscribed ERATO MUSE OF LYRIC POETRY.
She's tarnished by bad air or else patinaed artificially,
oh my silence, and stood for all my boyhood on a pedestal
beside an unplayed grand piano in our unused lace-curtain
    living room.
I'd grab her by the neck and ankles when I got her alone
and pump her up and down as if she were a dumbbell
to get some muscle, while a sunbeam turned the room's
dust particles into star-ways possibly out of there
and the silence of the instruments: the piano, me, and her lyre.
I made a way out loud, unlike the piano and the statuette.
They stand there forever dead silent in the dead silent living room
where nothing moves except the sunbeam and the dust in the
    sunbeam.
The lace curtains might move, but only in their own wind
or in the solar wind, because the windows to the avenue are
    nailed shut
to the traffic leaving Brooklyn for New York and the Wild West.

SPEECH FOR AUDEN

You were out when I called.
The bottles under the sink
are proof of ecstasy enough
to show that you are working
but divorced again. Why
litter the floor with phrases?
  "Spiritual mushrooms" I thought
quite good; the rest, interesting.
You American poets die
of alcohol, America, and lies;
of self-parody, bad sex,
Academia, and crankiness,
so do try to be pure
in your functional insanity,
and lock your door:
remember me.

RETRACTION

I gave up Art because
Art is lewd (Chaucer),
Art is immoral (Tolstoy),
and Art is useless (Rimbaud),
and went off slaving in
the Ethiopia of the Id
to buy my soul.
Ah what lewd immoral
useless things I did
to you, sweet love, before
you bit my hip off.

Now I've hobbled back
to where the battlements
of Wall Street rise
to sell my True Confessions
in the name of Christ,
transfigured into pure prosthesis
as the carrion bird
that Yeats saw on a coin
and advertised as golden.

FEBRUARY TWELFTH BIRTHDAY STATEMENT

That nameless son of a bitch of a critic who
wrote that I only wrote one good poem in
my life might be right so here's to you
future brother and sister and other poets
to drink to me and you with a shot
of bourbon and a bottle of beer
to the success of my intention on
my sixty-fifth birthday and to your
matching accomplishment. One poem
is enough. What have you two done,
my birthday mates Abraham Lincoln
and Tadeusz-Thaddeus Kosciuszko,
to get a Lincoln Memorial and a Kos-
iosko Street in Brooklyn? Nothing
but revolutionary activity. That son
of a bitch of a critic has said it: I have
made one poem, not the Gettysburg Address,
and not the military fortifications at West Point.

POEM

After your first poetry reading
I shook hands with you
and got a hard-on. Thank you.
We know that old trees
can not feel a thing
when the green tips burst
through the tough bark in spring,
but that's the way it felt,
that's the Objective Correlative
between us poets, love:
a wholly unexpected pain
of something new breaking out
with something old about it
like your new radical poems,
those audible objects of love
breaking out through nerves
as you sweated up on stage,
going raw into painful air
for everyone to know.

SPRING SONG FOR *SYMPLOCARPUS FŒTIDA* AND ME

Any plant that makes its own spring
is the plant for me: that's why I am for
the skunk cabbage in the New Jersey swamps.
Its hot frost-thawing fart-gas
makes a hole in the snow late in February
and it comes up like a purple prick
with a hairy brown foreskin around
its base in the slush, and does it stink.
It's a great thing to see and smell on a raw day:
you can tell yourself: maybe I can make it too
for another spring, if this lousy stinkweed can do it.

Wer, wenn ich schriee, hörte mich denn aus der *Engel*
Ordnungen?
Who, if I cried, would hear me out of the *Angel*
Orders?

      Nobody. Berryman was right.[1]
       You *were* a jerk. There *are*
       no *Angels*. Especially Kraut
       angels dressed up in Nazi
       uniforms giving wing Heils.
       They'd have to get *Ordnungs*
       to answer your jerky cries,
       so it's lucky you didn't cry,
       but just said "*if* I cried,"
       and used your life on great poems
       like *Sonnets to Orpheus* who
       didn't exist either, but so what?
       Berryman was wrong, really.
       You weren't really a jerk.
       Berryman was really a jerk
       to say a thing like that.

[1] See Berryman's *Dream Song 3*,
line 13: "Rilke was a *jerk*."

PRETRIAL HEARING

I thought she was a liberated woman
until I helped her in her kitchen
for our Faculty-Trustee Brunch.
Her big supply-side husband
kept on throwing sweeties,
honeys, darling baby dears
at her like bad old-fashioned
feather-boas which she didn't
want to wear but couldn't,
politely, duck, so she just
shrugged her shoulders as she
fiddled with the cocktail blender,
on and off, while going Pouf!
to me. She winked and smiled.
I thought I knew what she
was up to: Splits! For me!
Wrong. Her husband kind of said:
I'll supply you with a fine
distinction: you served once
in her kitchen. Wow.
I am always boss in her bed,
so shove off, Professor:
thou art too coarse to love.
You mind my grocery store.

MOCK TRANSLATION FROM THE GREEK

Both Erato the Muse of Lyric Poetry and Mime
and Apollo the God of Poetry and Music
are said to be with us, in us, above us, and behind us,
and are often figured to be with a lyre, one
singing and playing with it, and the other
having it at her feet and waiting for action.
If you try to beat him in an arts contest, he'll
skin you alive, the way he did Marsyas, that satyr
who was arrogant enough to challenge him once,
so you have to say, "God, let me have second prize
for my work, after you." Then he might nod,
if you're lucky, he might not even notice you,
if you're lucky, and if you do not listen to HER
when she comes up and talks in your ear,
whether kissingly or bitingly or just breathing something,
and if you don't listen and remember everything she says
or what you think she says, and get it all down,
anytime, anywhere, no matter what else is going on,
oh she will go away, either sadly, or amused, or furious,
or else with no human feelings at all, and leave you
with a mute in your mouth and a bug in your ear,
so you won't be able to hear her saying as she goes away,
    "You know
you stink. What you smell is your own upper lip.
It has to go. Take your last human breath of it, animal.
I'm telling your god Apollo to come down after you."

ON A MYTH.
ON A CONVENTIONAL WISDOM

Who has more fun in bed, men or women,
Zeus asked Tiresias, who had been both,
and when Tiresias answered, Women, of course,
Zeus got so mad he blinded him, he broke his bones,
he sent him back down to earth as a Theban seer.
and you know what happened to Thebes: Pfft!

It was a classic masculine response: We men
have less fun than women in bed, we can't
have children, we can't even have the pleasure
of suckling them, so we go around with empty looks
on our faces looking for excitement, ecstasy, revenge,
we blind people, we break their bones, we destroy Thebes.

This is the classic masculine response, this
is the conventional wisdom, this, we hope, is the myth.

GARGOYLE'S SONG FOR THE WARMING TREND

I am a sewer
useless to myself.
The water of this life
flows in and out of me
the wrong way. No drinks,
while I cry thirst,
no gutter jokes! I puke with it.
I'm all mouth.
Please be my house.
I'll vent your pipes and drains
and sing and roar for you
through the coming rains.

ON A FALLEN STATUE FORBIDDEN TO THE WOMEN AT POMPEII

I was the only man in the world
because I had no tits,
a permanent hard-on and
a prick as big as I was, so I
got packed in sculptor's clay,
holocaust alive in bronze,
and set up in a garden in Pompeii
with a tube run up one leg
and out my cock so I
could come forever to
all comers and flowers
with the fertilizing waters of Vesuvius
as an image of the god, Priapus.

PERVERSE EXPLANATION FOR
MUTILATED STATUARY

Her hair was made of poisonous snakes
and her mouth was an open scream,
so when they put their pricks in it
they had the feeling of having come
into nothing at all but a scream,
and the feeling of having been stung
all over. Then, as her teeth closed,
and they opened their eyes to stare,
they turned dead white and froze.

How else did they get there,
set up around Medusa's crypt,
those white statues of sound
young men with the missing pricks,
or with fig leaves over the wound?

ON A SUMMER GODDESS WHO SHOULD
BE NAMELESS

There are two things you have
to worry about about her.
She opens up for you
and she closes up on you,
but you shouldn't worry
too much about it because
this is the way she is
and this is the way you are:
You just shouldn't mention her name.
She loves you in her own way
and you love her in your own way
but you should never call her an ox.
If you call a woman an ox you're dead,
so what do you say about a goddess?
She might keep you alive, and in her own hell,
so you have to sweet-talk her to death, your own,
and call her by all sorts of names
like ox-eye daisy, dog-dayes-eye,
gold flower, white flower, clear flower,
Chrysanthemum leucanthemum or *Bellis perennis!,*
anything to avoid it, the name
of the ox-eyed goddess, the one
whose name begins with an H,
has two letters, E and R, and ends in an A,
you know the one I mean,
the one who comes on Midsummer Night
protected by and running that dog,
Sirius, to oversee the crisis
of opening and closing time:
that's when the flowers start

to bloom themselves to death
so that their seeds can blow away
and start up someplace else,
so watch it: do right by her
and her daisies. Beware the dog:
He's called Rusty or Red Dog
or else Blackie or Black Dog because:
If he looks down at you
out of one of his red eyes
if she happens to ask him to
as they swing by overhead,
you and yours and your whole countryside
will be wholly burnt up to black ashes.

NIGHT SCENE BEFORE COMBAT

There are trucks going down our street tonight
in convoy. The window rattles. There are lights
going on and off in the sky
beyond the suburbs, accompanied
by noises that sound like thunder.
I should be with them but
I try to get some sleep
with you. Did you know
that Metaphor means Truck
in Modern Greek? Truck. Carryall.
It figures. As William Blake said,
Eternity is in love with us
creations of time, and you *know*
about love, not just the weapons and battles,
but the problems of supply, logistics,
of getting the material to the front,
to the precise point of fire, in trucks,
at that point of place, at this point in time,
when the lights are flashing on and off
and what might sound like thunder is
not thunder, not thunder at all.
I should go downstairs and join
my outfit, I should get back
to the truck I left idling
by the curb, but I turn to you
for one last time in sleep, love,
before I put my uniform back on,
check my piece, and say So long.

POEMS SEVEN

(New poems)

● ● ● ● ● ●

NOMENCLATURE

My mother never heard of Freud
and she decided as a little girl
that she would call her husband Dick
no matter what his first name was
and did. He called her Ditty. They
called me Bud, and our generic names
amused my analyst. That must, she said,
explain the crazy times I had in bed
and quoted Freud: "Life is pain."
"What do women want?" and "My
prosthesis does not speak French."

AGAINST THE TEXT "ART IS IMMORTAL"

All art is temporal. All art is lost.
Go to Egypt. Go look at the Sphinx.
It's falling apart. He sits
on water in the desert and the water table shifts.
He has lost his toes to the sand-
blasts of the Saharan winds
of a mere few thousand years.
The Mamelukes shot up his face
because they were Iconoclasts,
because they were musketeers.
The British stole his beard
because they were imperialist thieves.
It's in the cellar of the British Museum
where the Athenians lost their marbles.

And that City of Ideas
that Socrates once had in mind
has faded too, like the Parthenon
from car exhaust, and from
the filthiness of the Turks
who used it as a dump.
If that city ever was
for Real in public works
and not just words he said:
No things but in ideas.
No ideas but in things
I say as William Carlos Williams said,
things as the Sphinx is our thing,
a beast of a man made god
stoned into art to guard the dead

from nothing, nothing and vanishing
toes first in the desert,
sand-blasted off into nothing
by a few thousand years of air,
sand, take your pick, picker,
go to Egypt, go look
at the Sphinx while it lasts.
Art is not immortal.
Art is not mortal.
All art is ideas in things.
All art is temporal. All art is lost.
The imperial desert is moving in
with water, sand and wind
to wear the godly native beast of man apart
back to the nothing which sculpted him.

And remember the Mamelukes, remember the Brits.
They were the iconoclasts of their own times,
primitive musketeers, primitive chiselers. This time
we can really blast the beast of man to bits.

DRUNKEN MEMORIES OF ANNE SEXTON

The first and last time I met
my ex-lover Anne Sexton was at
a protest poetry reading against
some anti-constitutional war in Asia
when some academic son of a bitch,
to test her reputation as a drunk,
gave her a beer glass full of wine
after our reading. She drank
it all down while staring me
full in the face and then said
"I don't care what you think,
you know," as if I was
her ex-what, husband, lover,
what? and just as I
was just about to say I
loved her, I was, what,
was, interrupted by my beautiful enemy
Galway Kinnell, who said to her
"Just as I was told, your eyes,
you have one blue, one green"
and there they were, the two
beautiful poets, staring at
each others' beautiful eyes
as I drank the lees of her wine.

POEM FOR ELLIOT CARTER ON HIS 90TH BIRTHDAY

I was walking behind Elliot Carter
up Eighth Avenue and saw that he
was waving his arms, and people looked at him
as if he was crazy, and he was
crazy: he was conducting the Juilliard
Chamber Orchestra soundlessly as it was
moving before him backwards seated
invisibly in formal black dress
as it performed his latest uncomposed piece
which he was composing slowly because
he writes slowly very slowly his wife
Helen always says and I say that he writes
for the performers not the audience
so that his music will go on
up the avenue for years and years
performed by the performers who
perhaps alone will hear it. So,
listen or don't listen, it will go on
playing anyway, invisibly unheard.

AMERICAN VARIATION ON HOW RILKE LOVED A PRINCESS AND GOT TO STAY IN HER CASTLE

She said that underneath the surface
of her beautiful skin and happiness
there was something she was scared of, it
could break out any time like hives, a
sense of loss, poverty, humiliation, or death.
Her beauty, children and three husbands
couldn't help her, and this is why
she married the Governor, the billionaire,
not because he was the governor but because
he had money and she needed money
to stop the terror, although the power helped,
and that I shouldn't hate her for this,
but understand her and love her,
so I did, and her husband gave me a grant,
not because I loved her or because
he was dyslexic but because
I was a good American poet.

ADDRESS TO A BIRD ON A VISIT HOME

"This is your brother the bird."
My mother made a kissing sound;
my dead father's voice spoke
from the old budgerigar's throat:
"Give us a kiss that's a good boy,"
through the static of his bird's wit.
Old brother bachelor, you are
too old and tame to fly away
to love, singing in the cold outside,
so imitate the hissing radiator
through your steam-heat age
and be my mother's husband
as I refused to be
and somehow got away.

COURTING SONG: ATTACK! ATTACK! ATTACK!

Oh I approached and bowed.
She turned away. I ran around
in front of her and bowed.
She turned away. I ran beside
her till she stopped. I bowed.
She turned away. I ran around in front
of her again and bowed and cooed.
Oh she lay down and sighed.
Then, Wham, Bang, Thank You Ma'am
I got her where she lived
and nearly died. I'm free,
God Love, again to be
whatever else I am besides
the dove of peace and pigeon for the day.

NOTE OF QUITS

Don't walk barefoot in the bathroom.
There was someone in the mirror who I killed.
God bless your hair-brush. God bless you.
Though I swept up as best I could,
there might be slivers of revenge left underfoot,
so watch out for intrusion, love: be shod.

WHAT IT REALLY MEANS

The cemetery where the college
students went to screw
was where we went to test
this S.M. business after
drinking up to it. I tried
to put a rose-thorn
through your ear lobe but
you ran off screaming while I
didn't feel a god-damned thing:
you weren't a masochist,
I wasn't a sadist, we
weren't even lovers, but
we did remain friends
back in philosophy class
where "The truth
of a theory is
demonstrated by
its practical application."
This is what it really
means, Pragmatism.

THE ESTHETICS OF CIRCUMCISION

She had one with a foreskin and
decided no more circumcisions,
it's not natural, I just love
the way the head comes out
for me, it's like a bud,
a flower, it's so
organic, organ, organismic, get it?
She walked around yelling at men
all night at the party, Are
you circumcised do
you have a foreskin. Quite a beauty.
When I asked her if it felt
better in there, who cares
how it only looks,
she yelled Fuck you Al,
and made as if
to kick me in the balls
while laughing really loud,
so I don't know.

BAREFOOT HOMILETICS, AFTER WITTGENSTEIN AND BOSWELL

Dew in the morning, dust at noon,
soreness in the evening, rest in brine.
Vertical soles all night, sideways
in colloquy, toes down in sex or up,
depending on the gender, depending on the case.
"The universe is everything that is the case."
Stubbed toes mean found rocks,
so all is detour to the tenderfoot
but traversible to callus. Calluses
are unshod graces, but a
bootless courage has its own
temerity. To strike a foot
with mighty force against a stone
is footless practice, and to say
"the universe is merely ideal"
is shoe philosophy, but
to watch your step is day
advice to the benighted since
feet have their feelings too.
So let the grass grow underfoot:
it tickles on the way to ground,
grass on the one side, roots on the other,
the balance of depths between.
That surface is falsely named
the surface. It is the case,
bare to the foot at the sole:
it is the top of the world
and the bottom of the sky to walk on.
So, seek water. Avoid the shod.

ANOTHER CAT POEM:
A CAT IS NOT A DANCER
BUT A HUNTER

The cat on its hind legs
taking a swipe at a mocking bird
was in a serious dance
but a stand-off dance
with the bird because
the cat didn't catch
the bird with its claws
and the bird didn't beak
the cat with its beak:
it just amused us,

but later the cat won some
other encounter. The words
"serious" and "dance" did not apply.
It came back to us wing-mouthed,
(the wings of a fledgling
coming out of both sides
of its mouth, the bird
a bloody fluff in its teeth)
expecting our congratulations,
expecting us to say Good hunting,
Dancer, dancer, oh you dancer.

THEY CALL IT "GRUMUS MERDAE"

It's good to be a burglar once in a while,
it makes your heart work better and improves
the circulation of the blood, money, and goods.
To break into somebody's house at night,
quietly, to wait until your eyes and ears
are fully open to the strange interiors
of other people's lives and rooms,
and then to burgle only what you find,
the silver and the television set especially,
the whiskey, the whiskey, and then leave,
but not before you have to take a shit,
it's good for the digestion and the disposition,
the cops call it a calling card but
it really is a neat joke on your victims,
you have to take a shit on the sofa,
it's a work of art on a cushion.

PROSE POEM

I was watching a building wall being knocked
down by a wrecking ball. During one swing of
the ball a man next to me took out a pocket mirror,
a pencil flashlight and a pair of tweezers. He held
the flashlight and the mirror both in his left hand
in such a way that the flashlight shined on his nose
while he could see his nose in the mirror. Then
he plucked something out of his nose, said Unkh!,
and put his tools away as the wrecking ball
hit the building wall and the wall fell.

WHEN I WAS DRUNK AND DISORDERLY THE BOSTON POLICEMAN TOLD ME:

Do not go to the Charles St. Jail.
You'll lose your shoes.
    "   "   " eyeglasses.
    "   "   " mind.
Lose my mind?
A crazy old man like me?
  "   "   "   "   " you.
Do not go to the Charles St. Jail.

Do not go to the Charles St. Jail.
You'll lose your pants.
    "   "   " false teeth.
    "   "   " ass.
Lose my ass?
A crazy old man like me?
  "   "   "   "   " you.
Do not go to the Charles St. Jail.

THE JACK-OFF OF THE GRAVEYARD SHIFT

When his machine was running right
he would come up behind you,
grab you by the elbows
and pretend to fuck you up the ass,
six-two, two hundred twenty pounds,
laughing, and you were helpless,
except for shouted words: Men
would tell him sexy things
to see him run to the john
and jack-off, yelling. Once
he wanted me to help him rob
the rich old lady in his rooming house
because he saw her pocket book
was full of folding money but
he jimmied the Coke machine instead
and disappeared. Later
the foreman said the cops
had been around the office after him. He was
a total innocent, a total fuck-up,
a natural for the graveyard shift
to liven up the nights of noise,
with the four-slide stamping-out machines
going 12-to-8, 12-to-8, 12-to-8,
sex-and-money, sex-and-money, sex-and-money.
He was missed. He kept people from going crazy too.
These stories were told about him for months.

SWING SHIFT BLUES

What is better than leaving a bar
in the middle of the afternoon
besides staying in it or else not
having gone into it in the first place
because you had a decent woman to be with?
The air smells particularly fresh
after the stale beer and piss smells.
You can stare up at the whole sky:
it's blue and white and does not
stare back at you like the bar mirror,
and there's What's-'is-name coming out
right behind you saying, "I don't
believe it, I don't believe it: there
he is, staring up at the fucking sky
with his mouth open. Don't
you realize, you stupid son of a bitch,
that it is a quarter to four
and we have to clock in in
fifteen minutes to go to work?"
So we go to work and do no work
and can even breathe in the Bull's face
because he's been into the other bar
that we don't go to when he's there.

HARD-ON DEATH

When what's-his-name the quadriplegic got
his final hard-on nurses came
from all around the Veterans Hospital
to ooh and ah and touch
it but it didn't do him any good:
he couldn't feel a god-damned thing,
and everybody got an extra joint
that night because he died, and joked
they should've run a flag up it, it
was his last salute to his cuntree.

IN MEMORIAM: DONALD MARK FALL

The Pope was riding a bicycle around inside
St. Peter's Basilica, not hitting any Catholics
or tourists, and looked around behind him
at me to see if he was being recognized. He was.
He had your face on, you dead dreamed lover.

This dream was much better than having that wet dream
of fucking Queen Elizabeth the Second when she
and I were both much younger and more sexual,
because now my libido is no longer royalist
but criticizes both religion and the Italian Papist
con game in a way that my mind agrees with

awake. The presence of your face however, is another
horrible problem: It means that my new old
dream self is an impotent homosexual necrophiliac
since you're dead, we're male, and I didn't come,
or else the face was the face of your suicide, devil,
so my libido believes in hell and is therefore religious.

Therefore I'll try to live for another ten years or so
in hopes I'll have the resolving third dream at 85
which will be a solid Marxist synthesis of the first two,
so that my dream self will pose it as a new thesis.
Death will come to me fleshed as a beautiful
democratic socialist communistic woman around his bones
and I will come to them for the last time in a healthy way.

THE MORNING OF THE DYING GIGOLO

I sleep in my girl's bed all day long
while she's out working. They think
I'm a professional because she keeps
me: they should hear her crying
when I wake her up to go to work.
They should see me when I go to shave
and don't. I come from bloody water as
I come from c(h)arnal dirt, and will not cut
my flower petals off for you, nymph,
since it's decided: I will go to the analyst.
Outside voices on the street will talk me
there and home,with love and love alone,
but not for you, Echo. This is Your
Narcissus saying now, and for the last time,
I WILL NOT ANSWER THE TELEPHONE.

FOR EUTHANASIA AND PAIN-KILLING DRUGS

As my father died of cancer of the asshole
the doctor wouldn't give him habit-forming drugs
for fear of making him a hopeless addict
so it took two men to hold him down to die.
I ran around like crazy to the bars that day.
When I got back that night they said he died at noon,
so I squeezed out two tears because they said I should.
Look at what happened to your Uncle John they said.
He couldn't cry when Grandpa died
so he went nuts and tried to kill the priest.
We had to have him put away for life
but you are blessed, you cried, a good son,
you are saved, oh you are not your father's asshole,
may you never rot in shit, God bless your come.

TOURIST POEM

Once I followed a drunken young gypsy
dressed in the performer's suit of lights
crossing the bridge from Sevilla
on his way home from performing
his debased act in some tourist trap.
He was singing or shouting, "Soy el diablo"
while two of his women behind him
were giggling and crying "Ay, que diablo El,"
and I wished I was the devil of the Book of Job.
How great it would be to be god's pet hood:
after going to and fro upon the earth
and giving boils and ashes to the rich
and doing what you god-damned please,
to be able to come back up to heaven
sure of the longest running show on earth
and the fullest attention of the greatest audience of one.

AGAINST VEILS
ON EXODUS 33:23 AND 34:33

When you invent an all-
powerful god, that god
is going to do you
something all beyond
your powers just as sure
as god mooned Moses since
your powers of invention are
so limited and his are not
limited,—-his are all-
powerful so he clowns
around: your shiny face,
after his ass is through
with it, will wear
the veil, the lying veil
of everybody laughing.
You are It, Mr. Mooned,
and you will make it so
that millions of masked men
war on the earth as believers
in you and your god saying
"and thou shalt see
my back parts: but my face
shall not be seen."
The veil is the lie
of the truth beneath it
and therefore corrupt.

PROTHALAMION OF QUANTUM MECHANICS AND ASTROPHYSICS
AGAINST THE TEXT "PHILOSOPHIA BIOU KUBERNETES"
(PHILOSOPHY THE GUIDE OF LIFE)

Part I: The Stutter of Quanta

It is impossible. The Uncertainty Principle
is Planck's Constant, 6.624 (or 5) times 10^{-27}
divided by two pis or more, more.
It is ridiculous, I am approximate,
we are either always flying apart and getting larger
or getting too close together in too small a way.
The intrusion of my gross instrument
distorts my knowledge of exactly
where you're at, you are so moving,
of exactly how you're moving where you're at.
Oh I can know your position but not
your velocity, your velocity but not your position,
and your position changes changes every time you make a motion.
You have to make a motion to take a position in this matter
and your position changes every time
you make a motion and your motions change,
and you are always taking up positions on my instrument
and making motions. I think
that you turn on and off.
You turn me off and on.
You part your wave
and wave your thing
at me.

       You part your thing
       at me
       and wave your part.

You part your part
and wave your wave
at me.
You wave and part
and part and wave
your thing and part,
waving,

         at me.

I withdraw inconsummate
if you are approximate,
I am empty, I
am in val-
id, I represent no
knowable abstraction if
I love you only because
you have no definite figure.
My love is incomplete in theory.
My love is uncertain in principle.
Whether you matter or
do not matter, whether
you are real or false,
I either love or am the law.
Therefore I will be as constant
as Max Planck's Constant in constant,
though divided in this farce
by two pis or more, more.

Part II. Dirge/Scherzo

In dreams I think
you are behaving like
my model universe
but know that you're
not sensible and that
you have a cloudy past,
no definite figure,
and are infinitely multiple,
divisible eternally,
but you are everything to me
so I want all of you
to be (Please be)
(considered as) my only one,
I want all of you
to be my only one.

What can I say as we go away
from one another, you and I,
except that I am not thoughtful,
that I am insensitive and imperceptive.
I don't even know if I could hope
that you and I could get together again,
or else slow down and find stability,
or simply go away forever, fast,
and leave me saying empty verse
out to an emptying universe:

Oh I don't know where you're going,
I don't know where you're at.
I don't know where you come from
or if you're coming back,
so tell me how I love you.

Part III: Antennae of Astrophysics and The End of Optics

I hear you after I see your light
and see you after I feel your stroke.
How you come on and then go off
without a sound, and then the sound
sounds. What struck me first,
and in the afterlight, and then,
when the noise came later, was
that touch, sounds and lights
must move at various speeds,
but speeds, and light is slow, slow:
we never see each other now,
but see each other either long
or just a little while ago,

so we live in one another's pasts,
you and I, and go into our own
futures all alone. We are always
moving apart and getting larger
and looking smaller, you in your
beautiful red shift, and me,

bug-eyed, observatory, shelled,
waving my antennae out at you
and flying away. I have my doubts
that I'm your metamorphic worm,
yolked in your egg of unknowability
and flying timewise to be born or burned.

IN FAVOR OF A FREE PUBLIC LIBRARY SYSTEM

Sometimes disturbed people go to the Public Library
and shout their secrets into the silence. One may shout
"They say I'm schizophrenic. What the hell does that mean?"
Or else "My husband says I'm frigid. How do I look that up?"
Then the readers look up from their reading, sanely disturbed
and often some well-read person starts talking quietly with them,
or else a compassionate librarian shows them the way to the catalog.
Then the library returns to the silence of its function:
the transmission of the words of the past in the presence
of the dust motes moving in the single sun-beam
coming down from the window to the check-out desk,
and if you think those dust motes are 'dancing like stars'
and are metaphors for some universal order or chaos
well, don't panic, keep quiet, don't start shouting
for meaningful advice from some well-read person:
ask a compassionate librarian to show you the way
to the American Poetry section where under 811 D or DUG
you'll find in my Collected Poems the palliative answer
to your stupid questions and the answer as to why
that liar Nietzche wrote "I don't like poets: they lie."

ANOTHER CAT POEM. TO A CAT PERSON

This is what your cat did to your mouse
while you were out shopping for what, cat food?
It carried it across your lawn in its mouth
and put it down under your flowering rose bush,
and watched it try to get away. It couldn't.
It must have had a broken back or hips
because it just scrabbled around going nowhere.
The cat gave it two quick smacks
with its claws retracted, to get some action,
but couldn't. Then it bit it in the back of the neck.
The mouse groaned with a bass human sound
and went limp. The cat gave me a look
of no significance except to signal
that it knew that I was there.
One drop of blood formed a thick hemisphere
on the mouse's neck. It was black or dark red.
Then the cat began to eat the mouse head first
instead of going for the easier belly or asshole.
I had always wanted to see the relation
of blood and roses restated in some novel way,
without the biological unconsciousness of thorns,
and here it was, established by the cat's
biological violence; I saw the color
of love and death exhibited red
in conscious and unselfconscious ways
in the mouse's blood beneath the roses.
'The mouse was the only groaner, the cat
was the only actor, I was the only witness,
the rose was only there, the thorn made its point
haha and this deposition was typed on paper,

not written in mouse blood by the thorn
on a rose petal and thrown into the Grand Canyon.
No. It is a poem made up to you, dear cat person,
to be published for love, publicity and money.

ON NOT WORKING AND THEN WORKING
ON WORKING AND THEN NOT WORKING

There used to be boring afternoons,
all quiet. The sun refused to set
or, no, the earth refused to move
so that the sun could set, yes.

Then time collapsed into itself. Days
ran through their cycles as machines, fast.
I said to myself hold on to yourself:
you could get spun off the earth, screaming.

I have to concentrate on three things
after work or during unemployment.
They are: birth, love, and death,
or else the horrors, rape, and suicide,

so that those loving couples on the streets
whispering their secrets of their own sweet time
should have it, and that bad dreams,
ideas, and bombers should not kill them.

THE SIGNIFICANCE OF CORN IN AMERICAN HISTORY

After the Puritans landed at Provincetown
and the women washed their dirty clothes
their men marched to Truro to perform
their first political act: theft.
They stole the Indians' corn
buried on Corn Hill, so why
is there no monument to them
or corn on Corn Hill in Truro?
For the same reason that there is no
working laundry in Provincetown:
Cleanliness is next to godliness,
thievery is next to Americanness,
and we must not publicize
that this country was made
by a bunch of dirty crooks.

I want to tear you apart.
I said to the butterfly,
in a sexy way,
and did, and it did
not matter: the tear
did not tear up the air
and rip the sky apart
the way it should
in a moral universe
because, you know,
morality is only human,
the universe and bugs
are not. I only made
a butterfly into a worm
like me. But oh
the wings, the wings:

Do not say these wings
are little frittilary fripperies.
They are great works of art
though small, say, compared
to the Milky Way, or you,
love in your various scales.
The great question is
why are they so beautiful
as the flying stained glass
flimsy windows of the worm's
evanescent flying cathedral.

CLOSING TIME AT THE SECOND AVENUE DELI

This is the time of night at the delicatessen
when the manager is balancing
a nearly empty ketchup bottle
upside-down on a nearly full ketchup bottle
and spreading his hands slowly away
from the perfect balance like shall I say
a priest blessing the balance, the achievement
of perfect emptiness, of perfect fullness? No,
this is a kosher delicatessen. The manager
is not like. He is not like a priest,
he is not even like a rabbi, he
is not like anyone else except the manager
as he turns to watch the waitress
discussing the lamb stew with my wife,
how most people eat the whole thing,
they don't take it home in a container,
as she mops up the tables, as the
cashier shall I say balances out?
No. The computer does all that. This
is not the time for metaphors. This is the time
to turn out the lights, and yes,
imagine it, those two ketchup bottles
will stand there all night long
as acrobatic metaphors of balance,
of emptiness, of fullness perfectly contained,
of any metaphor you wish unless
the manager snaps his fingers at the door,
goes back, and separates them for the night
from that unnatural balance, and the store goes dark
as my wife says should we take a cab

or walk, the stew is starting to drip already.
Shall I say that the container can not
contain the thing contained anymore? No.
Just that the lamb stew is leaking all across town
in one place: it is leaking on the floor of the taxi-cab,
and that somebody is going to pay for this ride.